WELCOME TRAVEL GUIDE

CITY OF MDINA
and
RABAT

The Cathedral – Mdina

WELCOME TRAVEL GUIDE

CITY OF MDINA
and
RABAT

John Manduca

with watercolours by
Cecily Napier

Publishers Enterprises Group (PEG) Ltd

Published by
Publishers Enterprises Group (PEG) Ltd,
P.E.G. Building
UB7, Industrial Estate,
San Gwann SGN 09, Malta

http://www.peg.com.mt
E-mail: contact@peg.com.mt

First published as
Connoisseur's Guide to City of Mdina, 1975
Second edition, 1981
Third (revised) edition, 1985

Revised and enlarged and first published as
Welcome Travel Guide: City of Mdina and Rabat, 2003

ISBN: 99909-0-336-0

By the same author

Welcome Travel Guide: Malta and Gozo
Guide to Harbour Cruises
Antique Maltese Clocks (Ed.)
Antique Furniture in Malta (Ed.)

Printed by PEG Ltd, Malta

To the memory of
EMMA AND CAMILLA

O much-loved city!

Many a tale is told
of thy great glories in the days of old.

Thou liest in silent sleep ...
Careless of all the hurrying hours that run,
Mourning some days of glory ...

Yet wake not from thy slumbers – rest thee well;
Rest thee well to mock all human greatness ...
Sleep in peace.

Acknowledgements

I have tormented friends and others with more knowledge than I can ever possess in preparing this travel guide.

I am particularly grateful to Cecily Napier – another lover of Mdina – for her attractive watercolours which give a flavour not usually associated with travel guides.

Change in the travel world is constant, but I remain grateful to those who supplied or checked information when the first impression was being prepared many moons ago: these include Mgr John Azzopardi, Dr Albert Ganado and Dr Paul Xuereb. I have now added new and up-to-date information which I trust will satisfy the most assiduous visitor to the Old City, and to its lively neighbour, Rabat.

Personnel at the Malta Tourism Authority, and especially Leonard Zammit Munro, have been helpful to a fault. The aerial view on the front cover and the photograph on the back, come courtesy of the Authority.

The Map of Malta is by the Survey and Planning Unit of the Planning Authority in Floriana. The Plans of Mdina and Rabat are by Polidano Press Ltd.

My children have been most helpful – Martin kept a watchful eye on Maps and Plans. John Napier helped with proof-reading – never my strong point. Three of my grandchildren, John-Paul, Matthew and Michael, were instumental in designing the front and back covers, and in solving computer problems which proved beyond me.

Photographs Nos 3 and 8 are by the late Anthony Cassar de Sain; Nos 4, 10, 13 and 14 are by Kevin Casha; No 5 is by the Malta Tourism Authority; No 11 comes courtesy of the Archpriest of St Paul's Collegiate Church in Rabat, and Nos 16, 20 and the Frontispiece are by Fr Michael Fsadni O.P.

Without the patience and understanding of my wife, Sylvia, it is doubtful whether this Travel Guide and its companions would have ever seen the light of day.

The author

Contents

List of Illustrations

Watercolours

Photographs

Maps and Plans

Introductory

Mdina is a gem of a bygone age. Peaceful and patrician, with its Spanish and Siculo-Norman palaces and churches, it is one of the few remaining mediaeval and renaissance fortified cities in Europe. Both its harmonious buildings and its atmosphere are unique. "No sooner has one set foot in Mdina, than time rolls back and one is in another age."

Inhabited since prehistoric times, and the Island's capital until 1568 when the Order of St John built Valletta, Mdina's history is as old and as chequered as the history of Malta. Mdina, also known as Notabile and Città Vecchia, has survived the vicissitudes of time and has preserved its own identity. It remains unchanged and unchanging, dreaming of the things it has seen during two thousand years. Long may it remain so, although there are disturbing signs of undue commercialism which, if left unchecked will prove disastrous.

The old City had been chosen as Malta's showpiece for Europe's Architectural Heritage Year held in 1975. Each year many visitors from all over Europe walk through its narrow, winding streets, sharing in its beauty.

This guide which includes neighbouring Rabat, will, I hope, add to their enjoyment. The delightful watercolours by Cecily Napier cannot fail to give added pleasure to the visitor.

"Beaulieu", Mdina.
October, 2002   JOHN MANDUCA

16th century map of Malta by Camocio which gives prominence to Mdina in the centre of the island

City of all time

The Mdina hilltop, almost in the centre of the Island, has been inhabited since man first came to Malta. The present city, one hundred and eighty-five metres above sea level, is believed to be the seventh, and there are beneath its ancient walls strata of six other settlements the first of which was a Neolithic village, perhaps five thousand years old. There was almost certainly a Bronze Age village on this site.

Phoenicians

The Phoenician adventurers found refuge in Malta's harbours and there is little doubt that this enterprising race spread inland, founding at least one settlement which would have stood on the site of the present city.

Romans

But it was the Romans (21 B.C.-A.D. 870) who made full use of the Mdina plateau and built a town which was some three times as large as present day Mdina. (See plan on page 32). Ptolemy (A.D. 127-58), the Greek Geographer of Alexandria, mentions four centres on the Island one of which was the city of *Melita* which was also the name of the Island. Cicero, Livy and Diodorus speak of stately buildings in the capital of Malta and of its rich style of architecture. Recent excavations have confirmed this.

The Mdina site was protected by steep cliffs on the east, north and north-east and was isolated on the south-west from the rest of the high ground by a ditch, hewn in the rock, which was crossed at two gates. The city walls were then over four kilometres in length and there is little doubt that the city, and indeed the whole Island, was prosperous. When in 70 B.C., Verres, the Roman governor of Sicily, plundered the Maltese shrine dedicated to Juno and robbed it of its ivory, Cicero denounced him. "I do not ask now", said Cicero, "whence you got those four hundred jars of honey, or such quantities of Maltese cloth, or fifty cushions for sofas, or so many candelabra ... but what could you want with so many Maltese garments, as if you were going to clothe the wives of all your friends?"

Abela, the Maltese historian, writing in 1647, noted the existence in many of the streets of Mdina of marble columns and statues, evidence of sumptuous Roman palaces and temples, including one dedicated to Apollo.

The bastion walls on the north, east and south of Mdina are mainly of Roman origin, while those on the west

The Walled Town

are Saracenic, with additions and alterations made by the Order of St John between 1530 and 1798. The Roman and Saracenic parts pre-date the invention of gunpowder and are vertical, while those built by the Knights of Malta are raised by a marked camber and were meant to withstand artillery fire.

It was during Roman period that Paul of Tarsus (St Paul) was shipwrecked here in A.D. 60 while on his way to Rome to face trial before Caesar. St Paul accompanied by St Luke – "our beloved Luke the physician" – was entertained for three days at the Mdina palace of Publius the head-man, whose father, Paul cured of "fever and dysentery" (Acts of the Apostles). Mdina's Cathedral stands on the site of the palace of Publius and Mdina has always been the See of the Bishopric of Malta. According to tradition, Publius was consecrated first Bishop of Malta, and St Paul is the patron saint of Mdina and indeed of Malta.

Arabs

The Arabs arrived in A.D. 870. For reasons of defence they reduced the capital city to its present size, (some 250 metres square) dug the moat which today defines Mdina's southern boundary, and changed its name to Medina.

Arab writers speak of the prosperity of the Island: "Melitah, island near Sicily, rich in everything that is good, and in the blessing of God ... well peopled, possessing towns and villages, trees and fruits ... it abounds in sheep and honey ..."

The Arabs introduced a whole range of new crops including cotton and hemp, improved methods of irrigation and are said to have introduced the lemon, the orange and the pomegranate to Malta.

Normans

In 1090, Count Roger of Normandy, a kinsman of William the Conqueror, landed in Malta and was hailed as a liberator as he entered the capital city. The Arab Governor sued for peace, which was granted on condition that the Arabs liberated their Christian slaves, paid yearly tribute to Roger, and aided him should he require their arms. On these conditions, the Muslims were allowed the free enjoyment of their own laws and their religion. (In 1224 however, the Arabs were expelled.)

Roger set about reconstructing the Cathedral of Mdina which had fallen into ruin during the Arab occupation, and the succession of Catholic Bishops, interrupted under the Arabs, was resumed. He divided the population into Barons, Nobles, Knights, Citizens, Burgesses and Rustics, and thereby introduced the feudal system into Malta.

It is interesting to note that a mass for the repose of the soul of Roger the Norman is still celebrated to this day on November 4th every year at the Mdina Cathedral.

Spaniards

Mdina increased in importance under the Normans, as well as under the succeeding Swabian House of Hohenstaufen (1194-1266), the Angevins (1266-82), the Aragonese (1282-1479) and the Castillians (1479-1530).

It was during this 'Spanish Period' that the old city achieved its special mediaeval and baroque flavour, its 'Siculo-Norman' buildings and its Spanish-style churches.

Unlike Valletta, the present capital, Mdina is not the creation of the Knights of St John. Sacheverell Sitwell in his book 'Malta' (illustrated by Tony Armstrong Jones) wrote:

"This is the island before the Religion dropped anchor in Grand Harbour. It is of an earlier date, and what is later in Mdina is kept within its own autonomy, as though it has an independence of the Knights. The inhabitants seem to have lived their lives in the shade of their own walls without depending on the Order ... In fact it was the old Spanish aristocracy that looked on the Religion with misgiving, that it was quick to defend its privileges reserved for it when the Emperor Charles V handed over the Island to the Knights, and that always resented their intrusion ... it is the old city of the island, and looked on itself as an outpost of Aragon and not an appanage of the Religion". (It is said that the inhabitants of Mdina continued to fly the flag of Aragon in defiance of the Knights of St John who arrived in 1530.)

Frederick III of Aragon visited Malta in 1355 and in 1432, a second royal visitor, Alfonso V stayed at Casa Inguanez (see page 40) seat of the doyenne of the Maltese Nobility. Nearly five hundred years later, in 1927, Alfonso XIII of Spain was likewise a guest of the Inguanez Family.

In 1428 Alfonso V had referred to the Capital as 'a notable jewel of the Royal Crown' *(Città Notabile della mia Corona),* and from then on the city was referred to as Città Notabile – the Notable City – in all official documents. Alfonso's visit no doubt boosted the morale of the inhabitants who were often prey to attacks by pirates and Muslim forces from North Africa. Invasions took place in 1412, 1422, and 1423. In 1429 Notabile was attacked by a considerable force of some 18,000 men operating from the Barbary Coast. Legend has it that the defenders were given new heart by an apparition of St Paul mounted on a white charger and brandishing an enormous sword. Be that as it may, the invaders failed to penetrate the capital city. (Mattia Preti captures this dramatic incidence in a large oil painting at the Mdina Cathedral entitled 'St Paul Conquering the Moors'. The painting includes an inset view of Mdina as it was prior to the earthquake of 1693.

The Spanish period saw the arrival of the great religious orders. The Franciscans came in 1370, the Carmelites and Benedictines (Nuns) in 1418, the

Augustinians in 1460 and the Dominicans in 1466. (The Jesuits came later in 1592). All these Orders had or have schools, churches and convents in Mdina or in the neighbouring town of Rabat.

Captains of the City

It was also during this period that the Island's Municipal Council or *Università* was firmly established to regulate the internal affairs of the city and of the island. An aristocratic body, its headquarters were at Mdina, first on the site of the Vilhena Palace (see page 36) and later at the Banca Giuratale (page 42). At its head was the Captain of the City or Captain of the Rod (*Capitano della verga*), so called because he was preceded on ceremonial occasions by a page carrying a rod of office (page 133).

Military service was obligatory from the age of sixteen to sixty-five and the Captain of the Rod appointed by the King was in command. He was assisted by four elected citizens known as Jurats (*Giurati*) and the *Università* had power to administer justice, to levy taxes and raise loans, to provide stores and provisions, to supervise weights and measures, and generally to make representations to the Sovereign on behalf of the people.

Knights of Malta

Although Alfonso V had promised that the Islands would be united "in perpetuity to the Spanish Crown", Charles V of Aragon broke this promise and in 1530 gave Malta and Gozo to the Order of St John of Jerusalem, "In order that they may perform the duties of their Religion and employ their forces and arms against the perfidious enemies of Holy Faith". The Knights, soon to be known as Knights of Malta, were the first of several international Orders of

Christian Knighthood founded during the time of the First Crusade. Their Constitution was sanctioned in 1113 by Pope Pascal II.

Defeated honourably in the Holy Land and in Rhodes, the Order was given Malta in return for a falcon presented yearly to Charles's Viceroy in Sicily and on condition, among others, that the Bishop of Malta would, continue to be chosen by the Emperor from three names submitted by the Order. The Order's Head was the Grand Master – twenty-eight ruled in Malta from 1530 to 1798 – and the Knights were divided into eight Langues or Divisions in accordance with their nationality. The Langues were those of Provence, Auvergne, France, Italy, Aragon, England and Germany. Aragon was later divided, making an eighth Langue of Castile and Leon. The Order has been described as, "an extraordinary organization, a cosmopolitan aristocracy, curiously combining the careers of monk and soldier of fortune".

The Knights accepted the gift (to which was added the liability of defending Tripoli) with reluctance. Nor was the reaction of the leading Maltese citizens, some of whom actually left the Island rather than submit to the jurisdiction of the Order, any more enthusiastic. The Bishop and clergy of Notabile were apprehensive.

Henry VIII's Nineteen Canon

When the Order of St John was forced out of Rhodes they wandered for seven years seeking a new home. Grand Master L'Isle Adam did the rounds of the Courts of Western Europe and visited London to see King Henry VIII, whose contribution was a gift of nineteen canon and one thousand canon balls. In 1530, the Knights having given up hope of returning to Rhodes accepted the offer by Charles V of Spain of the island of Malta. King Henry wrote to the Grand Master congratulating him on the acquisition.

In her "Malta of the Knights" (1929), Elizabeth Schermerhorn wrote: "to the educated and aristocratic Maltese, well informed on local history, the memory of the imperious Order that took away their parliament and free institutions, interfered with the sacred bishopric, snobbishly refused membership of the sons of families whose titles of nobility ante-dated the occupation of Rhodes ... is simply not to be discussed or defended in well-bred circles".

But there was no ready alternative, and the Grand Master, L'Isle Adam, a Frenchman, arrived in Grand Harbour with his followers on the 20th October 1530.

Soon after, L'Isle Adam made his way to the capital and swore at the gates of the City to uphold all the 'privileges, liberties and usages' of Notabile. He remained in the capital for over a week staying at Palazzo Falzon (see page 54), but many of the promises were soon forgotten.

Although Mdina does not owe as much to the Order as other towns and cities in Malta, nonetheless the Knights did greatly enhance its strength and beauty. The Grand Masters were great builders and every artifice of bastion, cavalier, counter guard, curtain and ravelin was planned for them by the foremost engineers of Europe.

"Malta became the emblem of the Order's temporal and spiritual power, and in its building were mirrored the grandeur and fanaticism, the piety and snobbery of this well-bred brotherhood. Fortifications, castles, palaces, churches and seminaries sprang up all over the Island almost overnight; complete new towns were planned, laid out and built in a matter of years".[1]

In 1551, Muslim forces, under the command of Sinam Pasha, landed at Malta, in what may have been a dress rehearsal for the Great Siege of 1565, and besieged Mdina. Sinam pitched his tents on the slopes of Mtarfa not far from the area known as *Qabar il-Lhud* (burial of the Jews).

---

[1] John Fleming in "Architectural Review", 1942.

A Nun's Vision

In 1551 the defenders' supplies were running low, the Vicar General was called to the Benedectine Abbey of Santa Scolastica (page 56) to speak to a nun who claimed to have had a vision. The nun said St Agatha had appeared and had advised that all the soldiers and citizens should walk in procession carrying her image which should be displayed on the bastion wall facing the enemy. The Vicar General acted on this advice and the Muslim forces, said to have been impressed by the number of the defenders, lifted the siege and attacked Gozo instead.

Maltese cavalry, 400 strong, under the command of Sir Thomas Upton, harried the invaders, and the siege failed. The Muslims attacked Gozo instead, carrying off most of the inhabitants into captivity.

During the next invasion, known as the Great Siege of 1565, when Soleyman the Magnificent, Sultan of Turkey, attacked the island with a force of 40,000 men, Mdina played a minor but, at times, decisive role. Apart from four companies of Militia, the island's livestock, those too old to fight, and the Order's horses and cavalrymen were sent to the Capital City. The Portuguese Governor, Don Mesquita, sent reinforcements at a critical time to besieged St Elmo and to Birgu, kept lines of communication open with neighbouring Sicily[2] and led enterprising cavalry charges on the Turkish base causing havoc and confusion in the enemy camp. Every morning, after the fall of St Elmo, "they hanged one Turkish prisoner upon the walls of Mdina".

When the Turkish forces finally started to withdraw from the harbour area, the Turkish commanders, in one last desperate effort, landed some 7,000 men at St Paul's

---

[2] A prominent courier was a Maltese, Toni Bajada.

Bay with orders to advance and take Mdina; but the dispirited enemy forces were driven back.

The Order whittled down the powers of the *Università*, and with the building of Valletta in 1568, Mdina declined in status. It became known as "Città Vecchia", the Old City. But emotionally it remained the centre of the Island.

During the reign of Grand Master Martin Garzes (1595-1601), a Spaniard, the Jurats of Città Vecchia, complained about the state of defences of their city and had to levy a special tax to carry out extensive repairs; these were taken in hand in 1600 and completed in 1616. Alarmed at the exodus from Mdina, Garzes granted the inhabitants the privilege of being tried in their own courts, of being exempt from military service, and of not being liable to prosecution for debt for a period of six years. These measures seem to have had some effect, though the decline in importance continued.

Military experts during the reign of Grand Master Jean Paul de Lascaris (1637-1657), decided that Città Vecchia would be untenable in case of a major siege and a decision was taken to dismantle its defences. Although this plan was never carried out, the brass cannon were removed and replaced by inferior iron pieces. The people objected, and when the Grand Master's men were dragging a heavy piece towards Valletta, the women of Mdina, perhaps thinking themselves immune from reprisal by reason of their sex, attacked them. Lascaris had many of them imprisoned. Already unpopular when he had ordered women not to wear masks in public during carnival time, this latest blow against the female sex earned Lascaris the hatred of the women of Malta and *Wiċċ Laskri* (face of Lascaris) became an expression of contempt which is used to this day.

In 1693, a great earthquake shook Sicily and Malta, and parts of Mdina including the Cathedral were heavily damaged. The re-building of the Cathedral started almost immediately but many other buildings remained in ruins and Grand Master Vilhena (1622-1736) inaugurated an extensive rebuilding programme, adding to the city's fortifications, and reshaping the entrance by moving the main gate slightly to the west. This movement made it possible for Vilhena Palace to be built immediately on the right as you enter the city.

Grand Master Martin de Redin (1657-1660) added bastions to the south wall (*Bastione di San Pietro*, and *Bastione del Palazzo*) and also fortified the bastion at the rear of the Cathedral. This was strengthened between 1739 and 1746 as was the great bastion next to the main gate built during the reign of Grand Master Ramon Despuig (1736-1741).

French

Napoleon ousted the Knights in June 1798. While the main body of French troops encircled Valletta, a column under General Vaubois advanced on Mdina where some troops still loyal to the Knights had retired in confusion. The city fathers were gathered at the Bishop's palace when they received a message demanding an immediate answer as to whether the French would be received as friends or foes. Unable to make effective resistance, the city council decided to surrender after having been given guarantees about their religion, their liberties and their property. The keys of the city were handed to General Vaubois, who was then invited to dinner at the Bishop's palace. These guarantees proved worthless.

The uneasy peace did not last long. The people were angered at the suppression of many of their monasteries and the confiscation of the greater portion of the silver plate belonging to the Cathedral of Mdina. When, on the 2nd September, representatives of the French Forces of occupation attempted to auction articles belonging to the Church of Our Lady of Mount Carmel (see page 52) the people prevented them from doing so. The arrival of

L' ANTICA CITTA DI MALTA, OGGI DETTA NOTABILE, RISTRETTA, E CINTA DI MVRA NEL SITO COMPRESO TRA LE LETTERE A.B.C.D.

Vittoriosa · Valletta · Notabile · Senglea

ARME DELLE QVATTRO CITTA PRINCIPALI DI MALTA

1. Cattedrale antico Palazzo di S. Pubblio.
2. Palazzo del Vescovo
3. Seminario
4. Convento, e Chiesa del Carmine.
5. Casa del Magistrato.
6. Armeria.
7. Monastero di S. Pietro.
8. Palazzo del Principe.
9. Curia.
10. Grotta di S. Paolo
11. Ove il S. Appostolo predicava
12. Tempio di Proserpina
13. Convento, e Chiesa di S. Agostino.
14. S. Francesco
15. Chiesa, e Convento di S.M. di Gesù
16. Convento, e Chiesa de PP. Domenicani.
17. Sito dell' antico Tempio d' Apolline

Mdina in 1772

30

Masson, Commander of the City garrison, to restore order did not help. He was attacked. Seeking refuge in the house of Notary Bezzina in nearby Rabat, he was hurled from the balcony and killed. The city was occupied by the insurgents, Church bells were rung, and messages dispatched to the various villages. In a few hours the revolt spread throughout the island and the French garrison retreated into Valletta. In 1800, the French surrendered to combined forces made up of Maltese forces and of British troops who had been called in to help fight the French.

British

Together with the rest of the Island, Notabile played its part during the Crimean war – when Malta was known as the 'Nurse of the Mediterranean' – the Great War, and World War II when the island was awarded the George Cross for bravery.

Under British rule, which lasted from 1800 to 1964, the old *Università* was abolished (in 1818) and the centre of power and commerce was firmly established in Valletta. Mdina retained its beauty, its peaceful inactivity and the ecclesiastical and aristocratic atmosphere of mediaeval Europe.

Malta became an independent state within the Commonwealth in 1964.

A city of all time.

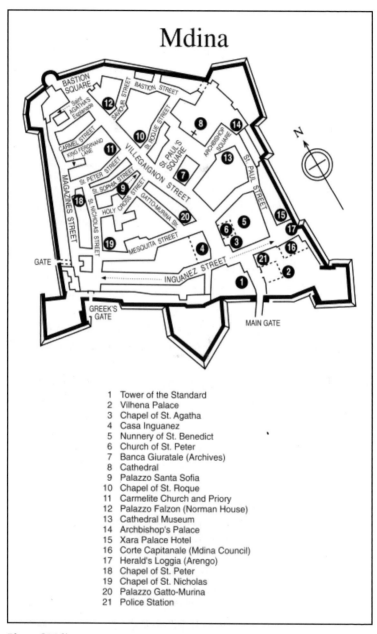

Mdina

1 Tower of the Standard
2 Vilhena Palace
3 Chapel of St. Agatha
4 Casa Inguanez
5 Nunnery of St. Benedict
6 Church of St. Peter
7 Banca Giuratale (Archives)
8 Cathedral
9 Palazzo Santa Sofia
10 Chapel of St. Roque
11 Carmelite Church and Priory
12 Palazzo Falzon (Norman House)
13 Cathedral Museum
14 Archbishop's Palace
15 Xara Palace Hotel
16 Corte Capitanale (Mdina Council)
17 Herald's Loggia (Arengo)
18 Chapel of St. Peter
19 Chapel of St. Nicholas
20 Palazzo Gatto-Murina
21 Police Station

Plan of Mdina

Tour of Mdina (1)

The Mdina Gate

Your tour of Mdina starts at the Main Gate. Constructed in 1724, with rusticated pillars and rich carvings, it replaced an older archway some distance to its right and is of an impressive baroque design. (Traces of the older gate are still visible).

The gateway bears an inscription recording the restoration of the city walls, and the arms of Grand Master Manoel de Vilhena (1722-1736), a Portuguese Knight.

It was here that successive Grand Masters were met by the Nobles of Mdina, and here that they swore to uphold their rights and privileges before being given the keys of the city. (See page 115).

On the inside of the gateway are bas-relief figures of St Paul, St Publius and St Agatha, protectors of Mdina and patron saints of the Island. Also here, are the arms of the City and of the Inguanez family – for many years Governors of Mdina – placed here by order of Alfonso V of Aragon. The Republican French removed these arms in 1798 and placed a statue of liberty over the gateway. The present escutcheon dates from 1886 having been replaced by order of the British Governor, General Sir Lintorn Simmons. (The latin inscription records the part played by Antonio Inguanez in quelling a rebellion which broke out in 1428).

Main Gate to Mdina, also known as *Città Notabile* and *Città Vecchia*

Tower of the Standard
St Publius Square (Mdina street map, page 32 – map reference 1)

On your left as you enter Mdina, is the Signal Tower of the Standard (*Torre dello Stendardo*) which dates back to the early 16th century when it replaced an older beacon tower known as *Torre Mastra*. From this tower, bonfires were lit to warn the rest of the Island of the landing of the enemy.

The watch-tower known as the Tower of the Standard

The arms of Grand Master de Vilhena were added when the Tower was remodelled.

The Police Station is in this little piazza, named after St Publius, which leads, as you turn left, into Villegaignon Street, the City's main thoroughfare. Previously called Strada Reale, and before that *Tal Muyeli* (Street of the gentry), it was named Villegaignon Street after Nicholas Durand de Villegaignon who defended Mdina against the Turks in 1551, and who helped to found Nouvelle Geneve in Brazil (renamed Rio de Janeiro after its capture by the Portuguese).

Before moving on, however, you may wish to visit and will certainly look at Vilhena Palace, opposite the Tower of the Standard.

Vilhena Palace
Natural History Museum (Mdina map, reference 2)

The graceful Magisterial Palace was constructed in 1730 by Grand Master Vilhena, who took advantage of the devastation caused by the earthquake in 1693 to rebuild the gateway, strengthen the bastions and generally carry out a programme of reconstruction. It was said of Vilhena that "he was not elected but was born a Prince"; his mausoleum in St John's Co-Cathedral in Valletta, reads: "Wherever you may be in these Islands, you will find monuments of his piety and munificence which made the Islands secure and attractive".

The site of the Magisterial Palace, (a Museum of Natural History, at the time of going to press) was formerly the seat of the *Università*, the Island's autonomous Commune. The first known building on this site to house the Commune was built in 1454; this was enlarged by Grand Master L'Isle Adam soon after the arrival of the Knights in 1530.

The Palace also incorporates the old Courts of Justice *(Corte Capitanale,* page 63), and the whole building,

Entrance to the splendid Vilhena Palace

including its fine ornate doorway, was designed by Charles François de Mondion, the Order's resident engineer. "The richly carved main door is faintly suggestive, with its banded columns, of the work of Phillibert de l'Orme. French too are the segmental-headed windows which mark the basement on each side of the main door, and the plan, an open courtyard with the palace set back around three sides of it and a screen occupying the fourth side, is reminiscent of many Parisian palaces".[1]

The Palace was used as a temporary hospital during a severe outbreak of cholera in 1837, as a military hospital for the treatment of eye diseases, and as convalescent home for British troops in 1860. In 1908 it became a hospital for tuberculous patients, being declared open by King Edward VII. It was named the Connaught Hospital after Edward's brother, the Duke of Connaught, who was then Naval Commander-in-Chief, Mediterranean. It was closed as a hospital in January 1956.

The Museum contains a growing collection of fossils, shells, insects, butterflies and birds. (The coat-of-arms of six holders of the Office of "Captain of the Rod" can still be seen in one of the rooms of the Museum.) Open daily in Summer 8 a.m. to 2 p.m. and in Winter Monday to Saturday 8.30 to 5 p.m., closing at 4 p.m. on Sunday. Entrance fee.

'Mdina Dungeons'

Next door to the Palace and, once forming part of it are the 'Mdina Dungeons'. Located in a 15th century prison; this is a veritable 'chamber of horrors' enacting scenes of torture, and execution prevalent in the Middle Ages. (Open 10 a.m.

---

[1] Quentin Hughes, "Fortress", 1969.

to 7 p.m. in Summer and 10 a.m. to 6 p.m. in Winter.
Entrance fee.)

Chapel of St Agatha
Villegaignon St (Mdina map, reference 3)

Turning left and then right into Villegaignon Street, you
will come across the small church of St Agatha. Originally
built in 1410 it was remodelled in 1694 to a design by

St Agatha's Chapel, first built in 1410

Lorenzo Gafà (1630-1710), a Maltese architect of renown who was also responsible for the design of the Mdina Cathedral. It has an altarpiece of the Saint by Giuseppe D'Arena, a Maltese artist of the 17th century. The remodelled Chapel was opened on June 26, 1695 by Bishop Cocco Palmieri in the presence of Grand Master Adrien de Wignacourt.

Legend has it that St Agatha sought refuge in Malta after fleeing from persecution in Sicily under the Roman Emperor Darius in the year 249.

Mass is celebrated once a year in this Church on the 5th February, the feast day of the Saint.

Casa Inguanez
(Mdina map, reference 4)

Casa Inguanez, to your left, is the seat of the oldest Maltese titled family. The Palazzo dates back to the 14th century though there have been various additions and alterations. The governorship of Mdina was almost hereditary in the family of Inguanez – (originally Desguanecks, from Catalonia, Spain) – Barons of Bucana (1350) and Djar il-Bniet (1695). The Island of Malta has had a nobility from the earliest times, though as present constituted the Nobility was founded by Count Roger the Norman in 1090. Titles consist of Barons, Counts and Marquises, and no title has been conferred since 1796. Precedent, always a ticklish business, is determined not by the degree of the title but by the date of creation.[2]

King Alfonso V of Aragon stayed at Casa Inguanez when he visited Malta in 1432; King Alfonso XIII of Spain did likewise in 1927.

---

[2] Titles of Nobility have not been recognized by the State since 1976.

Notice the striking door-knockers both in Villegaignon Street, where you now are, and in Mesquita Street round the corner to your left.

Nunnery of St Benedict
(Mdina map, reference 5)

Opposite the Inguanez Palace is the austere Nunnery of St Peter. The Benedictine community was founded in 1418 and the building had previously been used as a Hospital for Women, dedicated to St Peter. The building was repaired in 1479 and substantially restored in 1625.

In 1575, the Convent was visited by Mgr Pietro Duzzina, an Apostolic Visitor sent by the Holy See to report on the religious state of the Maltese Island. Mgr Duzzina found fifteen nuns, many of whom could not write. He laid down new rules, insisting that girls under the age of sixteen could not be taken in as novices and that one year's novitiate was essential before taking the veil. The rules of

The War Years

Mdina was relatively untouched by the 3000 or so air raids during World War II, despite having Ta' Qali airfield next door. But some bombs did fall on the walled City, one of which damaged the Benedictine Nunnery and killed two nuns.

In May 1941, at the height of the blitz a large parachute mine landed just below Bastion Square but did not explode. The whole of Mdina was evacuated while the Bomb Disposal Squadron tried to render the monster harmless. Fortunately they succeeded and the inhabitants of Mdina returned to the homes and air raid shelters.

Bombs which did explode fell in St Publius Square (near the Main Gate), the bastion next to Greeks Gate, Inguanez Street, Palazzo Falzon and the Benedictine Nunnery.

41

the Order remain very strict. No man is allowed into the Nunnery without the permission of the Bishop; the only exceptions are the doctor and the whitewasher, who in days gone by and in time of infectious diseases, would apply whitewash, which contains lime, to disinfect the walls. No nun is allowed out of the Convent, and up to 1974 this rule applied even after death: nuns were buried in a crypt within the Convent walls. There are now some ten nuns who spend their time in prayer and contemplation, in embroidery and in tending the convent garden.

Church of St Peter
(Mdina map, reference 6)

The Convent Chapel of St Peter is as old as the Nunnery of St Benedict but was extensively restored in 1625. Its altarpiece of the Madonna and Child with St Peter, St Benedict and St Scolastica is by Mattia Preti (1613-99). One of the leading artists of the 17th century, Preti was born in Calabria, Italy and was known as 'Il-Cavaliere Calabrese'. He settled in Żurrieq, Malta in 1661, and produced a large number of excellent paintings.

Banca Giuratale
(Mdina map, reference 7)

As you proceed along Villegaignon Street, you will pass by Casa Testaferrata on your right. (Observe the door-knockers). This impressive house is the seat of the Marquis of San Vincenzo Ferreri, a title created by Philip V of Spain in 1716. (This and the Benedictine Nunnery are believed to be the site of a Roman temple to Apollo).

Opposite is where the Knights of Malta had their armoury, and this is one of the areas in Mdina which saw action during the initial stages of the revolt against

A wrought iron street lamp

Napoleon's troops in 1798. ("We had to combat enraged lions", General Vaubois was later to report to his master). On your right, corner with St Paul's Square, is the imposing Banca Giuratale, built in 1730, which housed the *Università* when the site of the old 'parliament' was used by Vilhena to build his Magisterial Palace (Vilhena Palace, page 36).

During the revolt against the French, the citizens declared a National Assembly and appointed representatives to treat with Nelson against the French. The Palazzo Giuratale was used as their headquarters. It now houses National Archives.

St Paul's Square

This is the city's main square. It has a pleasant harmony and Renaissance flavour. To your right, facing the Cathedral, is the Banca Giuratale and the House used by

43

A Gold Hoard

On April 12, 1698 a little boy, Ignatio Parnis, got the surprise of his life when, rummaging in the soil in front of the Mdina Cathedral he came across a copper urn. In it were over 2,600 gold coins dating back to the Saracen period. These were probably hidden when news was received that Roger the Norman had landed and was heading for the capital city. The gold hoard soon became a disruptive issue between the Bishop and the Grand Master. The matter was referred to Rome and the Vatican, through Pope Innocent XII, decided like Solomon, to divide the spoils between the two claimants; the Cathedral Chapter used the welcome windfall to help rebuild the Cathedral.

The copper urn is now at the Cathedral Museum.

the Chief Magistrate. To your left is Casa Gourgion, and next to it an example of Victorian Gothic.

Prior to 1693 St Paul's Square was one third of its present size. Some time following the great earthquake the damaged houses in front of the Cathedral were cleared in order to form the present piazza.

The two brass cannons in front of the Cathedral were returned to the City from the Artillery Museum at Woolwich in 1888, through the good offices of the Governor, General Sir John Lintorn Simmons (1884-1888). The gun to the left, as you enter the Cathedral was manufactured in 1681, and the one to your right bears, among other inscriptions, the arms and motto of the House of Savoy.

The Cathedral
(Mdina map, reference 8)

The magnificent Cathedral of Mdina is, traditionally, said to have been built on the site of the Palace of Publius, "the chief man of the island" in Roman times. It was here

The Baroque Cathedral which dominates the city

that St Paul converted Publius to Christianity (*see appendix*).

It is possible that a church dedicated to the Blessed Virgin had stood on this site from the 4th century. Neglected during Arab rule (870-1091), it was re-built and generously endowed by Roger de Hauteville soon after his arrival in Malta in 1090. Enlarged in 1420, the present Cathedral, dedicated to St Paul, was built in 1697-1702 after its Siculo-Norman predecessor had been severely damaged by an earthquake in 1693. Part of the apse and the choir were re-built using stones taken from the derelict chapel in the Abbey of Santa Scolastica (see page 119). Designed by Lorenzo Gafà it is architecturally splendid in every way.

Quentin Hughes, sometime Professor of Architecture at the Royal University of Malta, writes: "The Cathedral dominates all other buildings. It is the most important work of the Maltese architect Lorenzo Gafà, and probably the finest domed church on the island ... The Mdina dome is Gafà's masterpiece; much bolder and more dynamic than anything he has attempted before ..."

The Cathedral was consecrated by Mgr Fra Davide Cocco-Palmieri, Bishop of Malta, on the 8th October 1702. It has always been the see of the Bishops of Malta, although prior to the arrival of the Order of St John in 1530, the titular Bishops frequently did not reside in the island.

The Cathedral Church has two impressive belfries with six bells, the largest of which was manufactured in 1643: the oldest, christened "Petronilla" was cast in Venice in 1370.

The Arms on the Cathedral façade, as you face the Church, are, left to right, those of Grand Master Perellos Y Roccaful (1697-1702), of the City of Mdina, and of Bishop Palmieri.

Two small attractive statuettes of St Peter and St Paul form part of the main central door.

The Cathedral is in the form of a Latin cross, 52 metres in length and 27 metres wide.

THE CHAPELS

The first chapel on the left aisle as you enter the Cathedral (see plan, page 48) has an altarpiece by Francesco Grandi (1831-1891), depicting the "Descent of the Holy Ghost", and two lunettes by the same artist representing the "Baptism of Christ" and the "Apostle Paul" preaching the Gospel.

The altarpiece in the second chapel represents the Madonna, as protector of Malta, the work of Pietro Gagliardi (1809-1890). Monuments to Bishop Publio Sant (1847-57) by the Roman Mario Gori, and a recent one to Archbishop Sir Michael Gonzi (1943-1976) are to be found here.

The third bay leads into the Sacristy. Observe the massive door, carved in Irish bog oak. This door stood at the main entrance to the Cathedral destroyed in 1693. Observe also the monument to Bishop Francesco Saverio Caruana, one of the leaders of the revolt against the French in 1798[3].

The Sacristy contains various pictures of interest, though not of outstanding artistic merit. Included among these is a painting showing Count Roger's arrival in Malta, by Francesco Zahra, a leading Maltese artist of the 18th century.

The third chapel, in the left transept, is dedicated to "The Annunciation". The painting is by Domenico Bruschi (1840-1910) of Perugia. Also here is a painting by Preti, depicting St Paul's appearance during the Saracen invasion of 1429 (See "City of all Time", page 19).

You come next to the Chapel of the Blessed Sacrament, to the left of the chancel. You will see, here, the famous Byzantine icon of the Blessed Virgin, sometimes attributed, wrongly, to St Luke. There is also a beautiful

---

[3] The other leaders were, Marquis de Piro, Count Manduca, Count Castelletti, Emmanuele Vitale and Vincenzo Borg.

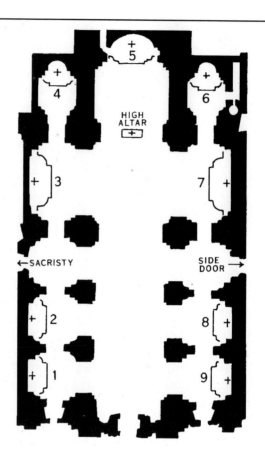

CATHEDRAL CHURCH OF ST PAUL
(Chapels and Altarpieces)

1 "Pentecost"
2 "Madonna and the Guardian Angel"
3 "The Annunciation"
4 Chapel of the Blessed Sacrament
5 Altar of the Choir
6 Chapel of the Crucifixion
7 "St Publius"
8 "Blessed Virgin and St Gaetano"
9 "St Luke and the Madonna"

Cathedral Church of St Paul

silver tabernacle which some attribute to the great Benvenuto Cellini (1500-71) the Florentine sculptor and goldsmith.

The painting over the altar of the Choir represents the Conversion of St Paul and is by Preti. The choir stalls date from 1481 and the inlaid figures of the apostles are from designs by Frederick Overbeck (1798-1869). The original older panels are in the Cathedral Museum (page 57). On the left hand side of the Choir is kept a fine 11th century silver cross. It was brought to Malta from Rhodes by the Knights, and is said to have been carried into Jerusalem by Godfrey de Bouillon in 1099. This cross is however not always on view to the public.

The handsome High Altar is inlaid with lapislazuli and other precious stones.

To the right of the High Altar is the Chapel of the Crucifixion. The beautiful crucifix carved in wood, is the work of Fra Innocenzo Petralia, a Franciscan. It was donated to the Cathedral in 1648, and was carried in procession through the Streets of Mdina in that year when the island was afflicted by famine. In the same chapel on the left is an interesting painting, of the Siculo-Catalan School, of St Paul.

The altarpiece in the chapel in the right transept is of "St Publius", by one of Preti's students. Two sepulchral monuments are to be found near the side entrance which leads onto Archbishop Square. One to Bishop Carmelo Scicluna (1875-85) by the sculptor Moschetti of Catania, and one to Cardinal Fabrizio Sceberras Testaferrata

A magnificent Silver tabernacle deserves special mention. This is only displayed on Maundy Thursday, in the Chapel of Repose. It was made in 1752 by Andrea Troisi and Annetto Pullicino and is an outstanding piece of craftsmanship. Do not miss if you happen to be at Mdina during Holy Week before Easter.

(1756-1843). Cardinal Testaferrata, a Maltese, was Apostolic Nuncio to the Swiss Republic during the years when Pope Pius VII was held prisoner at Fontainbleau.

The altarpiece in the next Chapel is of the "Madonna and St Gaetano". Lord Strickland of Sizergh, Count della Catena, and Prime Minister of Malta from 1927 to 1932 is buried here. His daughter, Mable Strickland, is also buried here.

"St Luke and the Madonna" forms the subject of the altarpiece in the last chapel in this aisle.

Flanking the main door is a statue of St Publius by Giuseppe Valenti of Palermo (1885) who was also responsible for the marble lecterns representing St Luke – who bears a striking resemblance to Garibaldi, and St John in the chancel; and a wooden baptismal font presented to the church by Bishop Giacomo Valguarnera in 1495. The marble statue of Queen Victoria in Republic Square in Valletta is also the work of Valenti.

The Church organ is Neopolitan and was made by Gio Domenico Ross in 1774. There is also another organ built by Coheman-Hart Church Organ Builders, U.K. in 1989.

The ceiling of the church is frescoed, with scenes from the life of the Apostle Paul, by Vincenzo and Antonio Manno (1794); the apse has a fresco of the shipwreck of St Paul by Mattia Preti; and the interior of the cupola was first painted by Gallucci in 1860, and completely re-done by Mario Caffaro Rore in 1956.

Recrossing St Paul's Square, we return to Villegaignon Street.

The Cathedral Museum is in Archbishop Square. This is described on page 57.

Palazzo Santa Sofia
Villegaignon Street (Mdina map, reference 9)

The groundfloor of Palazzo Santa Sofia, on your left and flanked by Holy Cross Street and St Sophia Street, is probably the oldest 'Norman' building in Mdina, although the tablet with the date 1233 may not be accurate. The first floor of the Palazzo was added in 1938.

The term 'Norman' in relation to buildings in Malta is used loosely to describe any house or Palace erected between 1090 when the Normans arrived and the cessation of Malta to the Knights of St John in 1530.

"The Medieval Maltese town-house was modest in size. It was built round a courtyard, and it faced out on to streets which were made purposely narrow to keep out the summer sun. The outside was severe, no doubt for reasons of security as well as climate, and the main decorative effect was provided by the delicate windows which helped to light the first floor, where the main rooms of the house were.

Palazzo Santa Sophia – the ground floor is said to be the oldest building in the city

The ground floor was devoted to stores, stables, kitchens and the like".[4]

Opposite Palazzo Santa Sofia is the Palazzo Gourgion, which served as a Seminary during the 18th century until the erection of the building which now houses the Cathedral Museum in Archbishop's Square.

Chapel of St Roque
(Mdina map, reference 10)

The little Chapel of St Roque was built here in 1728. It originally stood at the entrance to the city and was known as 'Santa Maria della Porta'. When the Cathedral was destroyed in the earthquake of 1693, church services were held there. It was demolished during Grand Master de Vilhena's replanning programme. The present chapel is popularity known as *Madonna tad-Dawl* (Our Lady of the Light). Its altarpiece is by the Portuguese painter Emmanuel Perren.

St Roque is the Saint who is invoked in times of physical disease, especially plague.

Carmelite Church and Convent
(Mdina map, reference 11)

The revolt against the French in 1798 started at the Church and monastery of Our Lady of Mount Carmel. It was the decision of the French Commissioners to sell by auction tapestries and other valuables of the church which signalled the start of the uprising, and the church bells sounded the alarm.

The Carmelites of the Old Observance, a Mendicant Order, came to Malta from Sicily in 1370 and established

---

[4] J.B. Ward Perkins F.S.A. "Medieval and Early Renaissance Architecture in Malta", 1942.

a Convent on the outskirts of Rabat. In 1658 they sought the protection of the City walls and were given a church known as *Santa Maria della Rocca* ("Our Lady of the Castle") in Mdina. This Church was subsequently demolished, and the present one built in 1659 to the design of Francesco Sammut; the Architect, Lorenzo Gafà was involved.

The belfry was destroyed by an earthquake in 1874 and was rebuilt a year later.

The Church has four chapels and seven altars. The altarpiece over the High Altar of the "Annunciation" is by Stefano Erardi, a Maltese artist.

Window in the Priory to Our Lady of Mount Carmel, where the revolt against the French started in 1798

The 16th July is the feast day of Our Lady of Mount Carmel, (celebrated on the last Sunday in July) and among the outdoor festivities organized by the Friars is a race for men and boys of all ages, which takes place in Villegaignon Street. The starting point is the Benedictine Nunnery and the finishing line, Bastion Square. An assortment of caps, hats, ties and belts are given away as prizes.

Palazzo Falzon
Norman House (Mdina map, reference 12)

The most complete of Mdina's mediaeval buildings, the Palazzo Falzon, commonly known as The Norman House, was built circa 1495 by the Aragonese Vice Admiral Falzon.

Grand Master L'Isle Adam was entertained here during his first state visit to Mdina in 1530.

Now a Museum, Palazzo Falzon contains an interesting collection of paintings, furniture and old Maltese silver. Observe the beautiful double windows, divided by slender colonettes, which are characteristic of 15th century Mdina, and the double line of pendant triangles which emphasize the string course. These graceful double windows are also to be seen on the Gatto Murina Palace, as well as in Carmel Street, St Peter's Street, Santa Sophia Street, Magazine Street and Inguanez Street. (See plan, page 32).

The management of Palazzo Falzon has been taken over by *Fondazzjoni Patrimonju Malti* (Maltese Heritage Foundation). It is being refurbished and will be turned in due course into a state-of-the-art Museum.

Bastion Square

We come now to the attractive Bastion Square, and to the corner house "Beaulieu" which incorporates part of the Benedictine Abbey of Santa Scolastica founded in 1494.

Palazzo Falzon

The nuns moved to a convent in Vittoriosa in 1604. Bastion Square had also been the site of a Jewish Synagogue until the expulsion of the Jewish community from Malta by order of King Ferdinand of Aragon and Queen Isabella of Castille in 1492. Until then, Jews played a prominent part in Maltese life, and had their own schools, hospitals and cemeteries.

The former firing-platform forming part of the *Bastione de Vaccari*, makes a good vantage point and the view from here, on a clear day, is magnificent. On the opposing ridge stands Mtarfa and the David Bruce Hospital. (Mtarfa was once the site of a temple to Proserpina, daughter of Zeus and Demeter, Queen of the Underworld). To your right, Mosta Church, built between 1833 and 1863 and said to have the third largest dome in the world.

Should you wish to return to the Main Gate the quickest way is to walk back along Villegaignon Street. But if you decide to see more of Mdina, you can follow the bastion wall which leads to Bastion Street and continue your tour of the eastern part of the City (Tour of the City 2). Alternately, re-cross part of Bastion Square and turn right along St Agatha's Esplanade for a walk round the western part (Tour of the City 3).

Tour of Mdina (2)

To the Herald's Loggia

As you walk along Bastion Street observe the small statue of Our Lord at the corner leading to Saviour Street. There once stood here a small 17th century chapel dedicated to the Saviour. Observe also how Bastion Street, like most of the streets in Mdina, while leading to the city centre, do not do so in a straight line. Most of the streets turn at intervals of ninety paces – the effective range of bows and arrows. Also for reasons of defence the width of the streets will allow for the passage of only one carriage or for a very limited number of armed men abreast.

At the corner with St Roque Street stands Casa De Piro and Casa Mifsud, both once used as a boarding school for girls (St Dorothy's Convent). In 1845-51, Casa Mifsud was the "Boarding School of St Paul's" run by the Jesuits.

In a tiny square is the entrance to a tunnel which leads to the 'De Redin' Bastion. It was from here that rebel forces, climbing the bastion wall, entered the city to help their Maltese compatriots oust the French in 1798.

As you re-trace your steps take the first turning to your left and you are back at the Cathedral. Cross over to Archbishop Square for a visit to the Cathedral Museum.

Cathedral Museum
Archbishop's Square (Mdina map, reference 13)

The Cathedral Museum, built by Bishop Alpheran de Bussan as a Seminary in 1733, ranks among the best

The Cathedral Museum

ecclesiastical museums in Europe. The Baroque design is attributed to Andrea Belli and the influence is predominantly Italian.

The Museum, which was until 1969 housed in the Cathedral buildings, owes its origin to a generous donation by Count Saverio Marchesi, a member of a Provencal family of St Tropez who settled in Malta early in the 17th century. On the right of the entrance hall is a bas-relief of the Count.

The Cathedral Museum comprises objects of art as well as Cathedral Archives, archives of the Inquisition and archives of the old *Università*.

Walking past the ticket office on your left, you will see displayed round the central courtyard, remains of Roman times and fragments of the old Siculo-Norman Cathedral including panels of the old choir dated 1481. Also here is a portable 18th century Neopolitan church organ which used to be carried in votive processions.

In the Parchment Room are documents of the Maltese

Commune, Papal Bulls, and a series of leaves of a mediaeval manuscript of the 11th century from works by St Augustine. Hanging on the wall are the Coat of Arms of the French Republic, placed over the Cathedral entrance during Napoleon's occupation in 1798, and the Coat of Arms of Charles V which surmounted the apse of the Old Cathedral (Restored in 1952).

We come next to the Musical Manuscript Room and the Mgr Gonzi Room. Mgr Sir Michael Gonzi was Archbishop of Malta from 1942 until his resignation in 1976. His carriage, cape and personal decorations are on display. (There is a statue of Archbishop Gonzi in the Cathedral. This Archbishop died in 1984 at the venerable age of 99).

In the next room is a small collection of church music mainly by Maltese *Maestri di Cappella*, as well as various manuscripts of religious and concert music by five generations of the Nani family.

Back to the corridor, and a visit to the recently arranged Mgr Psaila Room. Mgr Carmelo Psaila – "Dun Karm" – was Malta's National Poet and the author of the National Anthem – "This Fair Land". The Room is a tribute to him and to other Church dignitaries who contributed to the Island's literature and cultural life.

Walk past the ancient Choir stalls and into the old Refectory which is now used for *ad hoc* exhibitions and the display of prints. The Refectory leads into the Ceramics Room with Roman and Punic specimens, fragments of marble statues and a fine Ceramic Dish from Urbino (early part of the XVI century).

The Numismatic Hall contains an extensive collection of coins from every period of Maltese history from the Phoenician to the British, as well as from States with which Malta has had commercial and political relations. Some rare specimens are on display.

You can now walk up to the Upper Floor, past the 18th century Sedan chair into the Vestments Hall.

On this first floor is a small chapel with five paintings by Antoine de Favray, (who came to Malta in 1744), depicting the Annunciation, St Francis of Paola, St John Chrysostom, St Peter, St Paul and St Charles Borromeo. The main body of the chapel contains a fine collection of old Church vestments and antiphonaries of the 16th, 17 and 18th centuries. Included among these is a studious work by King Henry VIII of England, "Assertio Septem Sacramentorium" (Paris Edition 1562). It is a reply to Luther's arguments and a defence on the teaching of the Catholic Church on the Sacraments and the Sacrifice of the Mass. It earned the King the title of "Defender of the Faith" by Pope Leo X. Soon after, King Henry divorced his wife Catherine of Aragon, and broke off relations with Rome.

Usually also displayed here was an outstanding collection of old church silver, including a set of fifteen silver statues consisting of the Madonna, the twelve apostles, St John the Baptist and St Matthew the Evangelist. These had been seized from the Co-Cathedral in Valletta by Napoleon. The Cathedral Chapter at Mdina were asked to ransom them for twice their weight in silver. This they did, and in part payment the French were given the silver frontal for the High Altar of the Cathedral. A new silver frontal was made in 1839. This silver collection is however no longer here but in the Cathedral where it is displayed on Christmas Day, on the Feast of St Peter and St Paul (June) and on the Feast of the Conversion of St Paul (January).

Two large rooms contain the Museum's Picture Gallery. On display here are a cross-section of works from the 15th to the 19th century. Artists represented include Eberhard Keil (1624-1687), Mattia Preti (1613-1699) and Antoine Favray (1706-1798). Pride of place is given to the 15th century Panel depicting scenes from the life of the Apostle Paul (Spanish School).

Also on this floor are three small rooms containing a

selection of Old Master Drawings, and a larger Hall with an outstanding collection of woodcuts by Albrecht Durer (1471-1521), and other well-known engravers of the early German school. The Durer woodcuts include the complete series of "The Life of the Virgin".

Well worth a visit.

Archbishop's Palace
Archbishop's Palace (Mdina map, reference 14)

The Archbishop's Palace in Archbishop Square dates from 1722 and was built on the site of a much older one also attached to the Cathedral Church, which had undergone restoration in 1682. Following the earthquake of 1693, the palace was partially demolished in order to make room for the present residence rebuilt by the Cathedral Chapter during the Bishopric of Mgr Cannaves.

Mdina has always been the seat of the Bishops of Malta who played a leading part in Maltese affairs. Both the Bishop and the Grand Inquisitor, who arrived on the Maltese scene in 1574, lost no opportunity in trying to extend and fortify their jurisdiction so that the Grand Master, although a Sovereign Prince, had to contend with two rival and powerful authorities. Friction between the three powers was constant and often bitter. The Captain of the Rod, whose powers had been reduced under the rule of the Order of St John, also played a part in this perennial power game.

The Bishop increased his supporters by conferring the First Tonsure on all those who wished to keep out of the way of the Order of St John, and thus practically absolved them from their allegiance to the Order. Numerous appeals and protests were made to the Pope about this practice. Fortunately for the Grand Masters, relations between the Bishop and the Inquisitor were often acrimonious so that one could be played against the other.

61

In 1720, for example, the Inquisitor, Mgr Antonio Ruffo declined to accompany the Grand Master Zondadari on his first state visit to Mdina as he had fallen out with the Bishop, Fra Giacomo Cannaves.

When Bishop Cagliares started to build an Episcopal Palace in Valletta, the Grand Master tried to stop it since the "growth of such a plant would cast a shadow" upon the jurisdiction of the Order in its own city. The Bishop countered that his fold extended "wherever his sheep might wander" and the dispute was referred to Rome. The Bishop was allowed to finish his Palace but, in order to remind him of the limits of his authority, he was not allowed to have dungeons as he had in Notabile.

When granting Malta to the Knights, Charles V had stipulated that the nomination of Bishops of Malta was to be in the hands of his Viceroy in Sicily. The Order was

Tommaso Gargallo, a Spaniard, was Bishop of Malta for thirty-seven years (1578-1614), and is said to have "tormented the reigns of three Grand Masters". His relations with the Inquisitor were not much better, especially since he had to contribute an annual pension towards the maintenance of the Inquisitor's table. It was when one Inquisitor ordered a notice to be posted on the doors of the Cathedral suspending him from his Episcopal duties (for refusing to pay part of his revenue to the Inquisitor), that Gargallo returned to Malta from Sicily, tore down the notices and attacked the deacon and chaplain who had nailed them to the door, and the clerk who had read the notice to the people. When the Canons declined to acknowledge him while under papal ban, Gargallo made some of them prisoners, and dragged them behind his horse-drawn carriage all the way to his palace dungeons at Vittoriosa! Not surprisingly, two of the Canons died and there was a public uproar. 600 *scudi* were awarded to the relatives of the unfortunate canons and, amid protests, Gargallo was summoned to Rome where the Pope ordered him to undertake a pilgrimage to the shrine of Monserrat and to erect a church (the Jesuits Church in Valletta) as a sign of his repentance.

bound to submit three names one of whom was to be a subject of the Spanish Crown. As a result, the Knights often looked on the Bishop as the agent of the King of Spain, just as they considered the Inquisitor to be a spy of the Pope. Both clerics, however, often acted as champions of the people of Malta and of the City of Notabile.

Turn right and walk along St Paul's Street. This will lead you to a charming Piazza and to the Xara Palace Hotel.

Corte Capitanale
(Mdina map, reference 16)

The Xara Palace (Mdina Map, reference 16) is a fifteenth century building, once the seat of the Moscati-Parisio family, and now a Hotel.

Opposite, is the Corte Capitanale which forms part of Vilhena Palace (see page 36) and which housed the Courts of Justice, presided over by the Captain of the Rod. It is now used by the Local Council of Mdina. The figures of Justice and Mercy and the inscription "Legibus et Armis" recall its former function. Beneath, there are still the dungeons and the execution cells, and an underground passage, now blocked, led to the Palace of the Archbishop at the back of the Cathedral.

Herald's Loggia
(Mdina map, reference 17)

Adjoining Xara Palace is the graceful Loggia from where the Town Herald read the 'Bandi' (Proclamations) issued by the *Università*. When this was done, a Notary recorded an entry of the document in the register of the Commune giving the name and surname of the Town Crier ('Banditore').

63

The Old Courts of Law – The *Corte Capitanale*

A 'Bando' read on the 11th September 1472, prohibited the importation of cattle from the sister island of Gozo. Other 'Bandi' laid down that wine cannot be sold except with a licence obtained from the tax-collector; and that all vendors should bring in their weights and measures for inspection; various others deal with the price of pork, veal, cheese and honey, with the washing of clothes in public fountains, and with the disposal of garbage.

A 'Bando' dated the 30th September 1560 promised a reward of 100 *Scudi* (about Lm10) for information leading to the murderer of Fra Pietro de Revere, a Knight of Provence: "if the informer is an accomplice he will be paid 50 *scudi*; in any case the informant's name will be kept secret".

The Herald's Loggia where proclamations were made in days of old

It was customary in this Square for a boy, usually the son of the Captain of the City, or some other notable of the City, to read an oration in Italian praising the Grand Master on the occasion of his state visit to Città Vecchia.

Inguanez Street leads back to the Tower of the Standard and to the Main Gate.

Tour of Mdina (3)

A walk to Greeks' Gate

The western part of Mdina has a special attraction; its cloistered calm and its narrow, winding, streets are a delight. You will come across various double windows, armorial bearings and attractive door-knockers.

As you start on your way back to the Main Gate from Bastion Square, turn right into St Agatha's Esplanade and proceed down a hill to Magazine Street. On your left, in King Ferdinand Lane, is the 16th century Casa Isabella with its well-restored double windows and on your right, a

Entrance leading to Greeks Gate

permanent exhibition on the Knights of Malta (entrance fee). At the corner with St Peter's Street you will see two more of those windows, and a third with elaborate tracery is in St Peter's Street.

St Peter in Chains
(Mdina map, reference 18)

The chapel of St Peter in Chains, built in 1580 and restored in 1617 is no longer in use, but is being restored. On your right are the storehouses (*Magazzini*) used for the storage of weapons and ammunition.

Proceeding along Magazine Street, cross St Sophia Street and Holy Cross Street (where the old prisoners are said to have been located) and you will come to one of the three gateways to the City commonly known as 'the hole in the wall'. This is of recent construction. When the railway station outside Mtarfa was built in 1890, the need was felt for a convenient exit for the people of Mdina. (The Malta railway which linked Valletta to Mdina functioned until 1931. See note on page 134).

Greeks' Gate

A few yards ahead of the gateway, is Greeks' Gate Square and Greeks' Gate, ("Porta dei Greci"), probably so called because a Greek colony inhabited the area. The Gate was restored and embellished by Grand Master Vilhena in 1727.

Chapel of St Nicholas
(Mdina map, reference 19)

Re-crossing the Square, proceed along St Nicholas Street. The chapel of St Nicholas was built in 1550 and re-built in

67

Greeks' Gate – the second entrance to Mdina

A 'Siculo Norman' window

1692 to a design by Lorenzo Gafà. It is to be restored. A short walk up Mesquita Street leads to the delightful Mesquita Square (formerly Piazza Celsi). To your left as you walk up are a number of early 17th century houses, one of which was occupied by the Captain of the City. (Here is located the 'Mdina Experience' and the Cremona Art Gallery)

Palazzo Gatto-Murina
Gatto-Murina Street (Mdina map, reference 20)

As you leave Mesquita Square, continue walking along Mesquita Street. On your right is Casa Inguanez. Notice the door-knockers and the family arms above the door. Pause at the corner to Gatto-Murina Street for a look at the Palazzo of that name. Built in the 14th century, the Gatto-Murina Palace has fine double windows with their sculptured hood moulds and the characteristics string-course. The Palazzo now houses the 'Tales of a Silent City'.

Proceeding along Mesquita Street you will come back to Villegaignon Street. Turn right past the Benedictine Nunnery on your left and, a short distance away, is the Main Gate.

1. Grand Master L'Isle Adam greeted by members of the Maltese nobility at the entrance to Mdina – relations with the Order were not always cordial

2. *Città Notabile* during the Great Siege of 1565 as seen by Matteo Perez d'Aleccio (1547-1616) – the old Cathedral damaged by the earthquake of 1693 is clearly visible

3. Palazzo Falzon where the first Grand Master to Malta was
   entertained in 1530

4. A narrow winding street in the old capital city

5. The main square of Mdina during a re-enactment of a display by troops of the Order of St John

6. The splendid dome of the Cathedral – a masterpiece by Lorenzo
   Gafa

7. 'Siculo-Norman' window at Palazzo Gatto-Murina

8. The Church and Convent of Our Lady of Mount Carmel where the revolt against the French broke out in 1798

9. Greeks' Gate re-built in 1727 by Grand Master Vilhena

10. *Città Vecchia*

A look at Rabat

As we have seen, Roman Mdina incorporated a good part of neighbouring Rabat (see Plan on page 82–83). This area was too large to defend and Mdina perimeter was reduced to its present size during the Arab occupation. The purpose was to afford greater protection to the capital city. Later, the Order of St John cut a ditch in the rock to isolate Mdina and make it easier to defend.

The *Qasgħa* Chapel in Rabat

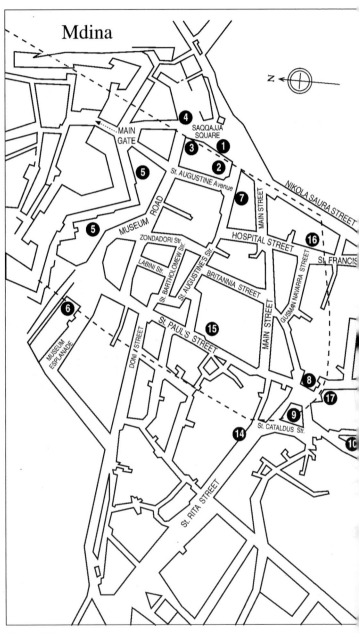

Plan of Rabat

Rabat

1. Bus Stop / Terminus
2. Bank of Valletta
3. HSBC Bank
4. Petrol Station
5. Howard Gardens
6. Roman Villa Museum
7. St. Augustine's Church
8. St. Paul's Church and Grotto
9. Police Station and Post Office
10. St. Paul's Catacombs
11. St. Agatha's Catacombs
12. Grand Hotel Verdala
13. St. Dominic's Priory
14. Bus Stop
15. Ta' Gesù Church
16. Franciscan Church and Monastery
17. Wignacourt Museum
- - - Line of Old Roman Walls

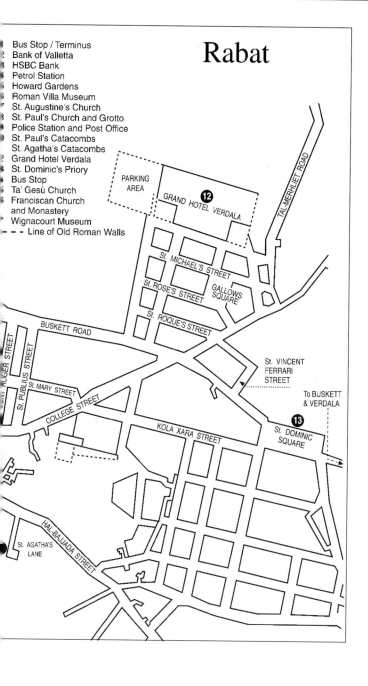

Rabat is now a suburb of Mdina and has expanded and grown over the years. It has a much large population than the Città Notabile with under 400 inhabitants. Rabat and its surrounding area are rich in archaeological remains including early Christian as well as pagan and Jewish catacombs. We shall visit some of the landmarks.

Roman House and Museum
(Rabat street map, page 82–83, map reference 6)

Walk out of the main Gate at Mdina, cross the Howard Gardens and turn right at Museum Road. Alternatively leave Mdina through Greeks Gate and turn right after crossing the ditch.

The ruins of this house were discovered in 1881. It was probably the town residence of a prominent Roman person. Mosaic floors were uncovered, and it was turned into a Museum with an interesting collection of busts of various emperors, sarcophagi and inscriptions.

Museum of Roman Antiquities

Reporting to his superiors in London the artist working for the *Illustrated London News* wrote in 1881: 'It is supposed by some to have been the residence of Publius (then Roman Governor of Malta at the time of St Paul's shipwreck). Mosaic floors of various colours have been unearthed. That in the foreground was white and black, while in the peristyle the pavement was red and green, and contained figures of a vase and of birds, and was surrounded by the remains of sixteen columns. The peristyle was twenty-four feet square ...'

The Museum is being given a face-lift and was not open for visits at the time of going to Press.

The National Archives
Santo Spirito Hospital (Rabat map, reference 16)

Originally known as the Hospital of St Francis, the Santo Spirito Hospital, which now houses the National Archives,

Santo Spirito Hospital, now housing the National Archives

85

A road in Rabat opposite Santo Spirito

was the first hospital to be built in the Maltese islands. It is to be found between Nikol Saura Street and Hospital Street (next to the church and convent of St Francis). It has an outstanding record of six centuries of use as a medical institution and was already in use in the fourteenth century. The Franciscan Friary to which it was attached was established in 1500. At its rear in Hospital Street one can see the 'revolving window' where infants who could not be cared for by their mothers because of dire poverty, were placed anonymously, and later taken to be cared for in the hospital.

St Paul's Church and Grotto
(Rabat map, reference 8)

From Saqqajja Square follow the signs through Main Street (*Triq il-Kbira*), turn left at St Paul's Street and walk into the Parish Square.

The Parish Church was remodelled at the end of the 17th century at the expense of a noble woman, Gusmana Navarra, to combine an earlier church built in 1575, and the adjoining church of St Publius constructed in 1617. The altar-piece in St Publius's church is by Mattia Preti, while that of the Parish Church is the work of Stafano Erardi (1678).

Attached to the church is St Paul's Grotto, where the Apostle is said to have spent part of his time in A.D. 60 following his shipwreck while on his way to Rome to stand trial. There are two altars in the Crypt, one dedicated to St Paul, with a marble statue by Melchiorre Gafà, and the other dedicated to St Luke (the physician who accompanied Paul on his journey). The inner part of the Crypt also has a marble statue donated by Grand Master Pinto, a Portuguese Knight who reigned in 1741-1773. The four bronze lamp stands in the inner Grotto are a recent donation from the inheritance of Pope Paul VI. The Grotto

The Parish Church of Rabat

leads to a small Christian hypogeum with various types of graves and an agape table.

In the Middle Ages the Grotto attracted many pilgrims from all over Europe. Admiral Nelson paid a visit in 1800 and Pope Paul II prayed there in 1990 during his first visit to the island.

Wignacourt College Museum
(Rabat map, reference 17)

An inscription in Latin over the main entrance to the Wignacourt College Museum reads (in translation): 'College of Brother Chaplains of the Order of St John of Jerusalem founded by Grand Master Fra Aloph de Wignacourt on the 1 February 1619'. Several alterations to the building have been carried out over the years, and it is now a fine Baroque Palace with a garden and small chapel. During World War II it was used as a hospital, a centre for refugees and a 'Victory Kitchen' when supplies were running low. There is a large air raid shelter which can be inspected, as well as a recently discovered catacomb.

Among the many treasures on display are two paintings by Mattia Preti, Our Lady of Sorrows and St Peter. A fine portrait by Cassarino of Grand Master Wignacourt, painted in 1617 is prominently displayed. There are many works by Maltese artists including those by Calì, Zahra, Hyzler and Caruana Dingli. Non-Maltese artists contribute a group of five Byzantine icons depicting the Virgin, the Virgin and Child, Christus Pasus, the Risen Lord and St Paul holding a scroll. Church vestments, a unique portable altar used on galleys of the Order, an elegant ebony cabinet inlaid with ivory and church organs are among the exhibits.

The Museum is situated next to the Parish Church and is open Monday to Saturday 10 a.m. to 3 p.m. (Entrance fee)

Wignacourt Museum, Rabat

Casa Bernard
(Rabat map, reference 18)

Casa Bernard, at 46 St Paul's Street (not far from the Church), is a 16th century house containing a fine collection of furniture, valuable paintings and other objects d'art. Viewing Monday to Saturday 10 am; 11 am; 12 noon and 1 pm or by appointment. Entrance fee. (Telephone 21444373 or 21451888).

Monastries

A number of impressive Monastries are to be found in Rabat.

The Dominican Priory

The Dominican Priory has a Baroque church (Map reference 13) and splendid Cloisters which may be visited. First built in 1455 on the site of an ancient shrine of 'Our Lady of the Grotto', the present Church dates back to the sixteenth century.

(A claim that an alabaster figurine of 'Our Lady of the Grotto' had shed tears was under investgiation at the time of going to Press; but already the statute is causing a great deal of interest among the faithful).

The Augustinian Church in St Augustine Street, (Map reference 7) was designed by Gerolamo Cassar in 1571. Cassar was the architect of St John's Co-Cathedral and of several of the Auberges in Valletta. The Franciscans in St Francis Street and the Minor Observants in St Paul's Street both have Baroque churches. The Church of St Francis (Map reference 16) was first built in 1400 but has since been restored while the Church of the Minor Observants was built around 1500, and restored a century later.

The Church and convent of St Augustine

St Paul's Catacombs
(Rabat map, reference 10)

Not far from St Paul's Parish Church are a series of Catacombs. The largest group is that of St Paul. The Rabat area contains pagan, Jewish and Christian catacombs and are distinguished by their sparse decorations: a Jewish tomb may have an incised seven-branched candlestick, while a Cross indicates a Christian burial.

The Catacombs

In 1530 Grand Master Philip de L'Isle Adam, granted a request to two persons to be allowed to search for hidden treasure on the island on condition that one third of the finds should go to the Order of St John and to the Church. This probably meant that the ancient cemeteries were plundered.

Chapel of St Cataldus

A steep flight of steps cut in to the solid rock with small graves for children leads into what was probably a large hall with, at both ends, the so-called agape table. This consists of a circular table with a bench at the same level, used for the funeral feast or wake. Passages lead off from these halls in several directions and into galleries of tombs. These catacombs were used as underground places of burial in the 4th and 5th centuries.

St Agatha's Crypt and Museum
(Rabat map, reference 11)

Further along Hal Bajjada Street are St Agatha's Catacombs which though not as large as those of St Paul are of interest specially because of the underground crypt dedicated to the Saint with frescoes the earliest of which belong to the 12th century, though the majority were painted around 1480 and are attributed to the Sicilian artist Salvo d'Antonio. It is intriguing to note that traces of much older frescoes belonging to the 4th and 5th centuries were discovered some years ago.

There is also a Museum with a fine collection of items which are insufficiently known. The Museum is open Monday to Saturday.

Beyond Rabat

Buskett

The woodland at Buskett, next to Verdala Castle were once used for hunting deer. Entrance is free and there are large number of citrus, pine and cypress trees. It is a delightful spot.

Some of the outdoor festivities surrounding the Feast of St Peter and St Paul (June 29, known locally as *L-Imnarja*) are held in Buskett Gardens when large crowds congregate, to eat rabbit, drink wine and listen to traditional folk songs. The Feast was so popular that women insisted they should be taken there, and to make sure their husbands did not forget, the undertaking was written into the marriage contract. An agricultural Show is also held at the same time in June.

Verdala Castle
(Rabat map, reference 13)

From the Priory of St Dominic's walk for a kilometre or so along Buskett Road.

Overlooking Buskett Gardens, Verdala Castle was built in 1588 by Grand Master de Verdalle as his Summer residence. The Castle has a chapel dedicated to St Anthony, Abbott.

The Castle was used in 1812 to house French prisoners

Verdala Castle built in 1588

of war, and was later turned into a summer residence for the British governors of Malta. It is now used by the President of Malta, and is not normally open to the public.

Inquisitor's Summer Palace

Not far from Verdala, in a locality known as Girgenti, is the attractive summer Palace of the Inquisitor. Built in 1625 by Mgr Honoratus Visconti, it has attached to it a chapel dedicated to St Charles Borromeo and was built in 1760 by another Inquisitor, Mgr Angelo Dusini. Recently restored and used by the government of the day – it was kept in readiness for possible use by President Bush of the USA and President Gorbachev of Russia during their Summit held in Malta in December 1989.

The Office of the Inquisitor was established by the Catholic Church to combat heresy, and was introduced into Malta in 1574, following a dispute between the Grand Master La Cassiere, a Frenchman, and the Spaniard, Mgr Martino Royas, Bishop of Malta. Out of the sixty-two Inquisitors who held office in Malta, twenty-five were subsequently made Cardinals and two became Popes. The Official residence of the Grand Inquisitor was in Vittoriosa; this is now a Musuem.

A member of the Falzon family (see page 54) was charged and found guilty, together with Antonio Manduca and others, of heresy by the Inquisition in 1575. The sentence included the confiscation of their property and land at Girgenti – on which the Inquisitor built his Summer Palace! Antonio Manduca escaped to Monpelier, became a Huguenot, and ended up as a Physician to Henry IV of France.

Dingli Cliffs

On leaving Buskett you can follow the signposts to Dingli Cliffs, a dramatic coastline and the highest spot in Malta – 700 feet above sea level – from where you get a good view of the tiny, uninhabited, island of Filfla, once used for target practice by the Royal Navy, and now a natural reserve.

You can also walk to the Neolithic temples of Ħaġar Qim and Mnajdra from here.

Cart Ruts

Nearby are a large group of cart-ruts. V-shaped grooves cut in the rocky terrain probably used as a means of transportation. Found all over Malta, the mystery of who built them and for what purpose remains unsolved. The tracks near Buskett are the most impressive on the island, offering a challenge to the imagination, and are known as 'Clapham Junction'.

The Big Cave (Għar il-Kbir)

Also in this area, south-west of Buskett, is the 'Big Cave' (Għar il-Kbir) which was inhabited up to 1836 when the farmers who used it were settled in nearby Siġġiewi mainly for reasons of hygiene. The size of the cave is unusual and its origin is thought to have been a dissolution pocket in the rock, the roof of which at some time collapsed.

According to one account some 27 families lived in these caves in 1647. "... every family had an area for itself, either a cave dug in by man, or one hewn by nature." A 17th engraving gives a Dutch artist's impression of life in this complex, and this is to be found in the Museum of Fine Arts in Valletta.

11. The shipwreck of St Paul by artist Stefano Erardi (1530-1716) – the altarpiece in the Parish Church, Rabat

12. The Wignacourt College Museum, Rabat – a 17th-century building

13. Part of the mosaic floor at the Museum of Roman remains, Rabat

14. The Catacombs in Rabat

15. The 16th-century church of St Dominic in Rabat, built over 'The Grotto of Our Lady' built in 1466

16. The Parish Church of St Paul in Rabat in festive mood. Below the church is the famous 'Grotto of St Paul'

17. Two items on display at Wignacourt Museum. *Left:* An 18th-century Maltese wall clock; *right:* a flower display made of gold and silver thread known locally as *Granutil*

18. Off to the market, with Mdina and Rabat in the background. A painting, circa 1925, by Edward Caruana-Dingli (1876-1950)

19. The Grotto of St Paul which attracted many pilgrims throughout the ages. Lord Nelson, on a fleeting visit to Malta, visited the Grotto and Catacombs in May 1800

20. The lovely courtyard and cloister of St Dominic's Priory

Practical Information

Hotels

Mdina

Xara Palace, St Paul's Square (Tel. 21454002). Five Star; 17 rooms.

Rabat

Grand Hotel Verdala, Inguanez Street. (Being re-furbished at time of going to Press).
Point de Vue – Guest House, Saqqajja Square (Tel. 21454117).

Eating out

Mdina

Bacchus, Inguanez Street (Tel. 21454981).
Caffè Medina, Villagaignon Street (Tel. 21451917).
Ciapetti's Bistro, St Agatha Esplanade (Tel. 21459987).
Città Vecchia, Bastion Square (Tel. 21451189).
De Mondion (Xara Palace Hotel) (Tel. 21450560).
Fontanella Tea Rooms, Bastion Street (Tel. 21450208).
Medina, Holy Cross Street (Tel. 21454004). Dinners. Closed on Sunday
Palazzo Notabile, Villegaignon Street (Tel. 21454625).
Trattoria AD 1530 (Xara Palace Hotel) (Tel. 21450560).

Rabat

Il-Veduta, Saqqajja Square (Tel. 21454777).
SB Grotto Tavern, Parish Square (Tel. 21455136).
Grapes, 1 Catacombs Street (Tel. 21450483).
Cafe San Paolo, St Rita Street (Tel. 21450865)
The Camps, Main Street (Tel. 21455109)

Banks

HSBC, Saqqajja Square, Rabat (Tel. 21454715).
Bank of Valletta, Saqqajja Square, Rabat (Tel. 21455966).

Post Office

Parish Square, Rabat

Bus Terminus

St Rita Street, Rabat (up to 9 a.m.) or Saqqajja Square, Rabat. Bus No. 80 and 81 get you to Valletta.

Sunday Masses

Cathedral, Mdina. 8am, 9.15am, 11am and 6pm. (Saturday at 6pm).
St Dominic's Church, Rabat at 6.00 am, 7.00 am, 8.30 am, 10.00 am and at 11.15 (English Language). (Saturday 6.30 in Winter and 7.00 pm in Summer)

Open Air Market

St Rita Street, Rabat, Sunday morning.

Police Stations

St Publius Square, Mdina (Tel. 21454531).
Parish Square, Rabat (Tel. 21454554).

What they said of Mdina

GIACOMO BOSIO, HISTORIAN

"Dell'Istoria della Sacra Religione" – 1602

"Our men hastened into the city and proceeded to fortify it by unremitting hard work (1551).

"The enemy knew the city well and realized that it was fortified by means of bastions and ditches only in the front part facing Rabat: it could therefore be successfully stormed by a large and well-formed squadron.

"The city has natural defences on its other three sides because it was approached by way of steep and precipitous crags and cliffs to its position on top of a prominent hill.

"The citizens of old had for this reason built neither towers nor observation posts not any form of fortification other than a single clay wall which was crumbling with age. Knowing this, the enemy decided to abandon the front of the city and to take it from the west where the hill slopes 200 feet towards the valley, and mount their attack from Mtarfa.

"Facing them, Governor Adorno, seeing the weakness of the wall ordered a ditch to be dug behind it ... he decided not to raise the inside embankment which served as a parapet because the cannon balls, striking the battery, might cause the ditch to be clogged up with falling masonry. With the help of the besieged citizens he had about finished his work.

"While the Governor Adorno was wondering which

course to pursue, the Bishop's Vicar, Giuseppe Manduca, went to see him to say that a holy nun from the new monastery (Santa Scolastica) claimed to have had a revelation from God the previous night that the Turks were about to besiege the city; but that if the marble statue of St Agatha which had already been brought into the city from her church in Rabat were placed above the observation post on the right side of the city gate in full view of the infidel, and that if a Mass were said to the glory of God and in honour of this blessed virgin and martyr, the city would be in no danger ..."

COMMENDATORE GIACOMO ABELA, HISTORIAN

"Descrittione di Malta" – 1647

"The city is no less famous for her origin and name than for her strength, courage and belligerence. This was amply demonstrated during various barbarian sieges, forays and invasions ... In all this she was defended by the efficacy of her arms as well as the protection of the glorious apostle St Paul her Father in the Faith and Titular Patron, and of her protectress St Agatha. The city combined valour with faith and devotion to her holy protectors who have on many occasions guarded and preserved her unharmed from the impious hands of the infidel. Her fealty and loyalty towards her princes and masters was equally great. But her greatest glory has been in her steadfastness to the Christian Faith from the day on which she was dedicated to Christ our Lord – as soon as the light of the newborn Faith was revealed to her by the great Doctor of the gentiles whom she had welcomed after shipwreck on our shores ...

"Today, however, more than in any other glorious epoch, she is fortunate to be living under the sign and standard of the Holy Cross of the Knights of Christ ...

"Endowed with such privileges and signal honours Notabile becomes the envy of every other city in Christendom.

"The ensign and arms of our city of Notabile consist of a shield divided vertically in two, one part white and the other vermillion: a clear portent of the future flag which would be hung up on her walls and fortresses. God in his wisdom having arranged that the happy journey of St Paul on Malta during which he planted the Christian faith should be followed by the event which was to become her greatest glory: the transfer to our shores of the Republic of our Holy Religion of Jerusalem and the raising thereon of its glorious banner of the white cross on a vermillion field, in order that this island might become the bulwark and bastion of all Christendom ..."

ABBE DE VERTOT, HISTORIAN

"The History of the Knights of Malta" – 1728

"The Grand Master, Villiers de L'Isle Adam, the council, and Chief Commanders got into the great port on the 26th of October, 1530, and as soon as they were landed, they went directly to the parochial church of St Lawrence, where having paid their first homage to Him whom the order acknowledge for its only sovereign, they went to the town, which is situated at the foot of the castle of St Angelo ... The Grand Master took up his quarters in the Castle; some days after his entry, he went and took possession of the capital, that lays further up the country, and about the middle of the Island. 'Tis called by Ptolemy *Melita*, after the name of the whole island; others give it the name of the *notable city*. We are told, that it was not 1300 paces in circumference; 'twas the usual residence of the bishop. The Grand Master, after his authority had been acknowledged by all the inhabitants, went thro' the whole island to find out a place

113

that might be safe, as well as commodious, for the settling of the council and whole body of knights."

P. BRYDONE, TRAVELLER

"A Tour Through Sicily and Malta" – 1773

"This day (June 7) we made an expedition thro' the island in coaches drawn by one mule each; the only kind of vehicle the place affords. We went first to the ancient city of Melita, which is near the centre of the island, and commands a view of the whole; and in clear weather, they pretend, of part of Barbary and of Sicily. The city is strongly fortified, and is governed by an officer called the *Hakem*. He received us very politely, and showed us the old palace, which is not indeed much worth the seeing. The Cathedral is a very fine church; and though of an exceeding large size; is at present entirely hung with crimson damask richly laced with gold.

"The Catacombs, not far from this city, are a great work. They are said to extend for fifteen miles underground; however, this, you are obliged to take on the credit of your guide; as it would rather be risking too much to put it to the trial. Many people; they assure us, have been lost from advancing too far in them; the prodigious number of branches making it next to impossible to find the way out again.

"From this we went to see the Bosquetta where the Grand Master has his country palace ...

"... We were delighted on our way back to the city, with the beauty of the setting sun; much superior I think, to what I have ever observed it in Italy. The whole of the eastern part of the heavens, for half an hour after sunset was of the fine deep purple, and made a beautiful appearance: this the Maltese tell us is generally the case every evening, at this season of the year."

MARCHESE CAMILLO STRETI, A NOBLEMAN OF RAVENNA

"Manuscript of a Knight of Malta" – (Edited by A. Macenzie-Grieve) – 1764

"Grand Master Pinto, while robbing the Maltese of their ancient civic rights and liberties, bestowed titles freely upon the middle class, encouraged social relations between the newly ennobled and the knights, and from many travellers' accounts – turned a blind eye upon closer and less legitimate associations. But the exclusive old Spanish families, whose admission to the Order was forbidden, aloof in their dark palaces in the old walled capital of Notabile (Mdina) would have none of the Knights or Noble. "The Barons are few" Spreti explains "and not tractable". Knights may be received only with the greatest difficulty into their homes, because they, having suffered various wrongs and discourteous treatment from the same, do not wish to expose themselves again to similar affronts, and thus it came about that many innocents must suffer for the bad behaviour of the guilty few ..."

GENERAL PASLEY

Diary, 1801

"I enter Città Vecchia, ascending by the road to the right and winding round to the only one gate that it has: Towards this part facing the north, it has a ditch and covered way but on the other parts looking down upon the low country are ancient high walls.

"This is built in the style of antiquity – the seat of the Bishop and College of Theology where every priest must study unless by special leave – expense their parents repine at. The high houses almost touch each other. The narrow streets wind in fanciful curves. It is very small.

115

"The church I had before seen, but not with so minute attention as I could wish. In the vestry is the picture of Roger the Gallant Norman, on a fiery horse. Upstairs are those of the different bishops who are nominated by the King of Naples out of three candidates appointed by the Governor of Malta. Seldom is a Maltese appointed as they have found in the few instances a disposition to aggrandize and enrich their own relations which is not the case in a foreigner.

"The present is Fra Vincenzo Labini, a Calabrian who has the right of appointing the clergy. Below are the vaults into which we descended with a light. In one of them are the bones of the dead treasured up in a corner and at the other end of the room the remains of some priest yet humid and in some degree of corruption.

"We hurried away from the shocking sight. As we ascended the stairs the melancholy sound of evening service increased the gloom of my ideas. After this we went to see the Courts where we found some of the Magistrates on their seats. They showed us the Tribunal of the Chief Magistrate who is called Captain of the Virga – a virga being carried round as a token of his dignity. He has four inferior magistrates – his assistants called Jurats. In a saloon adjoining are pictures full length of the Grand Masters who have successively commanded since the foundation of this building.

"The next object was the Curia: an extensive building with a court in which at present four companies are quartered. One clerk was then employed."

LOUIS DE BOISGELIN, KNIGHT OF MALTA

"Ancient and Modern Malta" – 1805

"The *Old* or *Notabile* City still preserves the name of *Mdina* among the inhabitants; this signifies city, and it was the only one at that time in the island. It is the seat of the bishopric: and its most remarkable edifices are, the palace of the Grand Master, built on the site of a fort taken down in 1455 by command of King Alphonso; and the Cathedral, erected on the foundation of a palace, which, according to ancient tradition, was inhabited by Publius, prince or protos of the island at the time of St Paul shipwreck.

"The body of the Cathedral has been rebuilt in a modern taste and is very little ornamented. The greatest part of the pictures are by Matthias Preti.

"The service of the Cathedral was performed by canons, chosen alternatively by the bishop and the Pope. The habit they wore in the choir was a purple *capemagne*; they officiated with a mitre, and wore a golden cross on the breast. The nomination to the deanery of this chapter was formerly a royal one; but it has since been transmitted to the grandmaster with all the privileges annexed to the Crown. Charles V in the act of donation, alone reserved to himself the right of choosing the bishop, who wore the grand cross of the Order, and held the first place in the council though the constitutional law of the Order did not acknowledge him for conventional bailiff.

"The Old City had for governor a *hakem* or *podesta*, chosen by the Grand Master out of the class of principal citizens. This governor bore the name of *captain of the rod*; because the sign of his jurisdiction was a rod."

ALEXANDER SUTHERLAND, HISTORIAN

"The Achievements of the Knights" – 1831

"Malta, according to the report of the commissioners sent to survey the islands was nothing better than shelterless rock of soft sand-stone called *tuffa*, six or seven leagues long, and three or four broad ... The *Città Notabile*, or capital, occupied a rising ground in the centre of the island,

and was a paltry, miserable and defenceless place. One side of the island was shelterless, and destitute of harbours, but another was provided with several of sufficient capacity to accommodate the largest fleet. The fortifications, however, that commanded them were insignificant, and in ruins ..."

G.P. BADGER

"Description of Malta and Gozo" – 1838

"Leaving St Antonio and passing through Casal Attard, where there is a fine Church, half an hour's ride will bring the traveller to the Old City, situation on one of the most elevated parts of the island, and nearly in its centre. It is surrounded with walls, and defended with bastions and other modern fortifications, which render it exceedingly strong. Before the arrival of the Arabs, a much more extensive space was enclosed within the walls, but it was diminished by them in order to render its defence more easy and practicable.

"In early times the city bore the same name with the island, and was called Melita according to Ptolemy the Geographer ... Upon the authority of Cicero and Diodorus Siculus we learn that the capital of Malta contained many stately buildings, and was very rich in the style of its architecture. This evidence is substantiated by several remains, which are still scattered about the city, and by the vestiges of ancient baths, and temples which have occasionally been found whilst excavating, both within the walls and about the suburbs.

Entry of Grand Master into Mdina

"On the election of a new Grand Master, the ceremony of inauguration was performed in this city. Early in the morning, the sovereign left Valletta, accompanied by his court and escorted by a bodyguard with bands of music. On his arrival near the city, he was saluted by the musketry and by the principal Giurato, who presented him with a bunch of artificial flowers, with an appropriate speech, and afterwards kissed his hand.

"The procession then proceeded, until it joined the Bishop and the clergy, who came out to meet them. The Grand Master was afterwards placed under a canopy borne on four poles by the *Giurati*, and continued walking until he arrived by the gates of the city, where a place was prepared for him to kneel upon, before which a cross was erected. After the gates were shut, the first *Giurato* stepped forward, bearing in his hand a silver dish, with two keys laid upon it of the same metal, and making a very low bow, addressed the sovereign in the following words:

"Most Serene Lord, the Divine Majesty has been pleased to favour us and this city, by placing over us so great a prince as lord and master; and the high honour is conferred upon me of presenting to Your Serene Majesty the keys of this city in order that you may take possession thereof. Therefore, my colleagues and myself, in all humility beg of Your Most Serene Highness to deign to swear upon the habit of the Grand Cross, that you will observe all the privileges, and franchises, and usages of this city, and of the island of Malta, which were conceded to them by the Most Serene Sovereigns of Aragon and Sicily, and by the magnanimous Grand Masters of this sacred Order of Your Most Serene Highness, and command that the same be observed."

"The Grand Master then laid his hand upon the cross on his breast, and said: 'I am bound to do so, I swear'. After the keys were delivered into his hand, the procession proceeded to the Cathedral, and after the celebration of mass, the pageant terminated."

WALTER H. TREGELLAS, Chief Draughtsman, British War Office

"Historical Sketch of the Defences of Malta, 1894"

"Città Nobile or Vecchia. When the Knights of St John arrived in Malta in 1530, Città Nobile was defended by weak and insignificant ramparts, ill armed. It is not known by whom, or at what precise dates they were erected; but there is a tradition that they occupied the site of still more ancient works, which were destroyed by King Alphonso.

"Città Nobile possesses considerable interest; not only on account of its being the seat of the Bishopric, and as containing some remarkable buildings, including the Palazzo Magistrale (built it is said on the site of an ancient fortress) but also on account of the valuable part which it played, as a citadel, during the siege of 1565. On this occasion a reserve force of the Knights issuing thence was the immediate cause of the raising of the siege; the Turks believing the small army which attacked their rear to be the vanguard of those succours whose arrival was daily expected from Sicily.

"The important part played on this occasion by Città Vecchia has caused most writers on the defence of Malta, down to the close of the last century, to attach some importance to the necessity of maintaining this post".

Tregellas, in an Appendix to his Historical Sketch, then quotes extracts from "Le Devis General des Fortifications de Malte" by the Chevalier Blondel, Engineer to the Order of St John, in 1618:

"Città Nobile. Commonly the Old Town ... It is the most ancient in Malta, and was for many years the only one.

"Blondel proposed certain reforms in its fortifications in 1659 which were not carried out, except the foundations of a low bastion between the right and left wings. This was completed without following Blondel's plans. It should be reformed in accordance therewith. It is doubtful whether this place should be fortified at all, but as it contains the residence of the Bishop of Malta, the Cathedral, Convents, and public buildings, and was moreover, of considerable service during the siege by the Turks, to say nothing of the miraculous intervention on that occasion of St Paul himself (its especial protection), Blondel thinks that its fortifications should be maintained."

WHITWORTH PORTER.

"A History of the Fortress of Malta" – 1871

"The Chief town called Città Notabile, lay in the centre of the island; and although surrounded by a rampart was barely capable of the slightest defence. The island in fact lay completely open to the piratical incursions of the infidel corsairs, who swarmed on the northern coast of Africa, and nothing could have protected it from their visits, save the utter and hopeless poverty of its inhabitants. Barely able to raise a few scanty vegetables from the ungrateful soil, they depended almost entirely on Sicily for the importation of grain, and this they obtained by the exchange of their cotton which they cultivated to a considerable extent ...

"In addition to the Città Notabile which was itself little better than a village, there were several other smaller villages called *casals* dotted over the island."

ARTHUR S. FLOWER, SCHOLAR

Notes on Renaissance Architecture in Malta, 1897

"Città Vecchia, or Notabile originally the chief city of the island, and the scene of St Paul's sojourn there, commemorated in the dedication of many religious buildings is exceedingly picturesque, both within and without. Its Romanesque Cathedral was destroyed by an earthquake about two hundred years ago, and its present grandly situated building, of which Lorenzo Gafà, a Maltese was architect, was consecrated in 1702. The wide nave, upwards of 36 feet in span, is noteworthy; also the carved and inlaid choir-stalls said to date from 1480, and very good in design and execution, the gorgeous altar-ornaments and other treasures which escaped the general pillage of the island by the French invaders in 1798."

D. H. LAWRENCE, AUTHOR

"Memories of the Foreign Legion" – 1924

"We went to the old capital in the centre of the island, and this is interesting. The town stands on a bluff of hill in the middle of the dreariness, looking at Valletta in the distance, and the sea. The houses are all pale yellow, and tall, and silent, as if forsaken. There is a cathedral, too, and a fortress outlook over the sun-blazed, sun-dried, disheartening island. Then we dashed off to another village and climbed a church-dome that rises like a tall blister on the plain ..."

SIR HARRY LUKE

"Malta – An Account and an Appreciation" – 1949

"... Mdina, described by Malta's chatty seventeenth century topographer and analyst, the Vice Chancellor Abela, as "placed like a navel in the middle of the island", has, as is natural, a quality somewhat different from the maritime cities created by the Knights around the harbours. It is, in the first place, much earlier in origin than these; secondly, it lies inland; thirdly, it crowns a hill. Not that all of it is medieval by any means; that elegant and ubiquitous builder, the Portuguese Grand Master Manoel de Vilhena, in the early eighteenth century repaired and strengthened the city's walls, rebuilt its impressive gateways that give access into the enceinte, and erected just within the Main Gate, whose approach bridges the moat, the graceful palace of the 'University' ...

"... But if not all of Mdina is medieval, there is nothing within its walls that is noticeably later than Baroque; and, were it built of ancient, narrow, weather-beaten brick and not of stone, it would recall one of the small hill-towns of Tuscany or Umbria ..."

SACHEVERELL SITWELL

"Malta" – 1958

"... One of the smallest and most compact of historic cities, and entirely and wholly complete within the circle of its walls ... No sooner has one set foot in Mdina, one has only to walk through this gateway, then time rolls back and one is in another age. It is the most sudden transition imaginable, and accomplished in a few paces and within a few seconds. Everything, the roads, the roofs, the sidewalks are of the same colour at all hours of the day. At the moment it is golden because of the sunset but at other times it can be butter coloured, from yellow farm butter to salted butter, or paler than that with, doubtless, variations of its own when there is full moon. Ideally, a posse of Capuchin monks comes out of a church door and goes off in perspective down a golden side street ...

"How quiet it must be at Mdina on a moonlit night! There are people, men and women, brought here by their naval duties, who will tell you it is the most beautiful little city they have ever seen ... Italian was made an official

123

language of the Religion in the seventeenth century, but Mdina is in many respects an old Spanish town. It is a Spanish culture ... It is the old city of the island, and looked on itself as an outpost of Aragon and not an appanage of the Religion."

Further Reading

AZZOPARDI, JOHN (Ed.), *St Paul's Grotto, Church and Museum at Rabat* (1990)

AZZOPARDI, JOHN (Ed.), *Mdina and the Earthquake of 1693*

BONELLO, GIOVANNI, *Art in Malta – Discoveries and Recoveries* (1999)

BROCKMAN, ERIC, *Last Bastion, Sketches of the Maltese Islands* (1961)

BRADFORD, ERNLE, *The Great Siege* (1965), *Paul the Traveller* (1974)

BLOUET, BRIAN, *The Story of Malta* (1967)

BONNICI, ARTHUR, *History of the Church in Malta* (1968)

BUHAGIAR, MARIO & FIORINI, STANLEY, *Mdina, The Cathedral City of Malta*

DE LUCCA, DENIS, *Mdina, A History of the Urban Space and Architecture* (1993)

ENGLAND, RICHARD & CONRAD THAKE, *Mdina, Citadel of Memory* (1995)

FIORINI, STANLEY, *Santo Spirito Hospital, The Early Years to 1575* (1989)

LAFERLA, ALBERT, *The Story of Man in Malta* (1935)

LUKE, SIR HARRY, *Malta, An Account and an Appreciation* (1960)

MAHONEY, LEONARD, *5000 Years of Architecture in Malta* (1996)

SCHERMERHORN, ELIZABETH, *Malta of the Knights* (1929)

Appendices

SOVEREIGNS FROM 1090 TO 1530

NORMANS:

Roger (Count of Normandy)	1091-1101
Simon (Son of Count Roger)	1101
Roger II (Son of Count Roger)	1101-1154
William I (Son of Roger II)	1154-1166
William II (Son of William I)	1166-1189
Tancred I (Son of Roger II)	1189-1194
William III (Son of Tancred I)	1194

SUABIANS:

Constance (Daughter of Roger II and wife of Henry VI of the House of Hohenstaufen)	1194-1197
Frederick I (Son of Constance)	1197-1250
Conrad I (Son of Frederick I)	1250-1254
Conradin (Son of Conrad I)	1254-1266
Manfred (Natural son of Frederick I)	1266

ANGEVINS:

Charles of Anjou	1266-1283

ARAGONESE:

Peter I (III of Aragon)	1283-1285
James I (Son of Peter I)	1285-1296

Frederick II (Son of Peter I)	1296-1337
Peter II (Son of Frederick II)	1337-1342
Louis I (Son of Peter II)	1342-1355
Frederick III (Son of Peter II)	1355-1377
Mary I (Daughter of Frederick III)	1377-1420
Martin I (Husband of Mary I)	1402-1409
Martin II (Son of Martin and Mary)	1409-1412

CASTILLIANS:

Ferdinand I (Nephew of Martin II)	1412-1416
Alphonso I (Son of Ferdinand I)	1416-1458
John I (Son of Ferdinand I)	1458-1479
Ferdinand II (Son of John I)	1479-1516
Joanna I (Daughter of Ferdinand II)	1516-1518
Charles (Son of Joanna and Philip of Austria, Emperor of the Holy Roman Empire)	1518-1530

GRAND MASTERS OF THE ORDER OF
ST JOHN IN MALTA

Philippe Villiers de L'Isle Adam (French)	1530-1534[1]
Pietro del Ponte (Italian)	1534-1535
Didier de Saint Jaille (French)	1535-1553
Juan de Homedes (Spanish)	1536-1553
Claude de la Sengle (French)	1553-1557
Jean Parisot de la Valette (French)	1557-1568
Pietro del Monte (Italian)	1568-1572
Jean l'Eveque de la Cassiere (French)	1572-1581
Hughes Loubenx de Verdalle (French)	1581-1595
Martin Garzes (Spanish)	1595-1601
Alof de Wignacourt (French)	1601-1622
Luis Mendez de Vasconcellos (Portuguese)	1622-1623
Antoine de Paule (French)	1623-1636
Jean Paul de Lascaris Castellar (French)	1636-1657
Martin de Redin (Spanish)	1657-1660
Annet de Clermont de Chattes Gessan (French)	1660
Rafael Cotoner (Spanish)	1660-1663
Nicolas Cotoner (Spanish)	1663-1680
Gregorio Carafa (Italian)	1680-1690
Adrien de Wignacourt (French)	1690-1697
Ramon Perellos y Roccaful (Spanish)	1697-1720
Marc' Antonio Zondadari (Italian)	1720-1722
Antonio Manoel de Vilhena (Portuguese)	1722-1736
Ramon Despuig (Spanish)	1736-1741
Manoel Pinto de Fonseca (Portuguese)	1741-1773
Francisco Ximenes de Texadas (Spanish)	1773-1775
Emmanuel de Rohan Polduc (French)	1775-1797
Ferdinand de Hompesch (German)	1797-1798

---

[1] In Rhodes from 1521.

INQUISITORS IN MALTA

Mgr Pietro Duzzina	1574
Mgr Pietro Sant'Umano	1575
Mgr Rinaldo Corso	1577
Mgr Domenico Petrucci	1579
Mgr Federico Cefalotto	1580
Mgr Francesco Costa	1583
Mgr Ascania Libertano	1585
Mgr Gio. Batta Patralata	1587
Mgr Paolo Bellardito	1587 & 1590
Mgr Angelo Gennai	1590
Mgr Giovanni dell'Armi	1592
Mgr Innocenzi del Bufalo (afterwards Cardinal)	1595
Mgr Antonio Ortensio	1598
Mgr Fabrizio Verallo (afterwards Cardinal)	1600
Mgr Ettore Diottalevi	1605
Mgr Leonello della Carbora	1607
Mgr Evangelista Carbonesio	1609
Mgr Fabio Delagossa	1614
Mgr Antonio Torniello	1619
Mgr Paolo Torelli	1621
Mgr Carlo Bovio	1623
Mgr Onorato Visconte	1624
Mgr Niccolo Herrera	1627
Mgr Ludovico Serristori	1630
Mgr Martino Alfieri	1631
Mgr Fabio Chigi (later Pope Alexander VII)	1634
Mgr Gio. Batta Gori Pannellini	1639
Mgr Antonio Pignatelli (later Pope Innocent XII)	1646
Mgr Carlo Cavalletti	1649
Mgr Federico Borromeo (afterwards Cardinal)	1653
Mgr Giulio degli Oddi	1655

Mgr Gerolamo Casanatte (afterwards Cardinal)	1659
Mgr Galeazzo Mariscotti (afterwards Cardinal)	1663
Mgr Angelo Ranucci (afterwards Cardinal)	1666
Mgr Carlo Bichi (afterwards Cardinal)	1668
Mgr Giovanni Tempi	1670
Mgr Ranuccio Pallavicini (afterwards Cardinal)	1672
Mgr Ercole Visconti	1676
Mgr Giacomo Cantelmi (afterwards Cardinal)	1679
Mgr Innico Caraccioli	1683
Mgr Tomaso Ruffo	1686
Mgr Francesco Aquaviva (afterwards Cardinal)	1690
Mgr Tomaso Ruffo (afterwards Cardinal)	1694
Mgr Giacinto Filiberto Ferreri	1698
Mgr Giorgio Spinola (afterwards Cardinal)	1703
Mgr Giacomo Caraccioli	1706
Mgr Ranieri Delci (afterwards Cardinal)	1711
Mgr Lazza Pallavicino	1718
Mgr Antonio Ruffo (afterwards Cardinal)	1720
Mgr Fabrizio Serbelloni (afterwards Cardinal)	1728
Mgr Gio. Francesco Stoppani (afterwards Cardinal)	1731
Mgr Carlo Francesco Durini (afterwards Cardinal)	1735
Mgr Lodovico Gualtieri (afterwards Cardinal)	1740
Mgr Paolo Pasionei	1743
Mgr Gregorio Salviati (afterwards Cardinal)	1754
Mgr Angelo Durini (afterwards Cardinal)	1760
Mgr G. Ott. Manciforte Sperelli (afterwards Cardinal)	1767
Mgr Antonio Lante (afterwards Cardinal)	1771
Mgr A.F. Chigi Zondadari (afterwards Cardinal)	1777
Mgr Alessio Falconieri	1785
Mgr Gio. Filippo Gallarati Scotti (afterwards Cardinal)	1785
Mgr Giulio Carpegna (afterwards Cardinal)	1793

(Mgr Carpegna went to Rome in 1798 and Rev. G.B. Gatt remained as Pro-Inquisitor. Two months later however, he was expelled by order of Napoleon Bonaparte).

BISHOPS OF MALTA SINCE 1530

Fra Balthasar Walkirk (German)	1530
Fra Tommaso Bosio (Italian)	1538
Fra Domenico de Cubelles (Spanish)	1540
Fra Martin Royas de Portalrubio (Spanish)	1572
Fra Tommaso Gargallo (Spanish)	1578
Fra Baldassare Cagliares (Maltese)	1615
Fra Giovanni Balaguer Camarasa (Spanish)	1635
Fra Lucas Bueno (Spanish)	1664
Fra Lorenzo Astiria (Spanish)	1668
Fra Michele Gerolamo Molina (Spanish)	1678
Fra Davide Cocco Palmieri (Italian)	1684
Fra Giacomo Cannaves (Spanish)	1713
Fra Gaspare Gori Mancini (Italian)	1721
Fra Paolo Alpheran de Bussan (French)	1728
Fra Bartolomeo Rull (Majorican)	1758
Fra Giovanni Pellerano (Sicilian)	1770
Fra Vincenzo Labini (Italian)	1780
Fra Ferdinando Mattei (Maltese)	1807
Mgr Francesco Saverio Caruana (Maltese)	1829
Mgr Publio de' Conti Sant (Maltese)	1847
Mgr Gaetano Pace Forno (Maltese)	1857
Mgr Count Scicluna (Maltese)	1875
Mgr Antonio Buhagiar (Maltese) (Administrator)	1885
Mgr Sir Pietro Pace (Maltese)	1889
Mgr Angelo Portelli (Maltese) (Administrator)	1914
Mgr Dom. Maurus Caruana, O.S.B. (Maltese)	1915
Mgr Sir Michael Gonzi (Maltese)	1943
Mgr Joseph Mercieca	1976-

CAPTAINS OF THE CITY

Capitano

Giacomo de Pellegrino	1365
Giovanni d'Aragona	1371
Guglielmo Murina	1372
Gulino Ricciari	1399
Francesco Gatto	1403-05
Francesco Giovanni de Santa Columba	1406-07
Diego de Portocarrero	1413
Diego Terrazza	1414-15
Lupo Terrazza	1415
Giovanni Lupo Terrazza	1416
Ruggiero de Serriano	1418
Paolo de Pellegrino	1428
Antonio d'Esguanez	1429
Francesco Gatto	1431
Antonio d'Esguanez	1433
Antonio d'Esguanez	1437
Francesco Platomone	1438
Antonio d'Esguanez	1439
Gerardo d'Esguanez	1440
Antonio d'Esguanez	1442-53
Carlo di Paternò	1454
Nardo di Bordino	1455
Stefano Pirrera	1456
Giovanni de la Xabica	1457
Pietro Giovanni di Mazara	1458-59
Pietro de Baldes	1460
Bartolomeo di Clementis	1461
Paolo de Nasi	1462-64
Raimondo de Parisio	1466
Giovanni di Mazara	1467
Trisfano du Guevara	1468
Giorgio de la Xabica	1470
Giovanni di Mazara	1471-72
Simone di Mazara	1473

Giovanni di Mazara	1474
Giorgio de la Xabica	1475
Giovanni di Mazara	1476
Simone de Mazara	1477
Giovanni di Guevara	1479
Giorgio de la Xabica	1480
Torres di Guevara	1481
Pietro de Ribera	1482-85
Simone de Mazara	1486
Carlo de Guevara	1487-92
Antonio Gatto d'Esguanez	1493-98
Giovanni di Guevara	1500-05
Giacomo Falzone	1513
Manfredo Caxaro	1514
Matteo di Guevara	1516
Giovanni di Mazara	1518
Luguterra de' Nava	1519
Giovanni di Mazara	1520
Pietro de' Staniga	1521
Leonardo de' Bordino	1522
Ambrogio Falzone	1523
Giovanni di Mazara	1524
Michele Falzone	1525
Pietro Falzone	1526
Giovanni de Nava	1527
Antonio d'Esguanez	1528-29
Leonardo Calavà	1530
Paolo de Naso	1531-32
Antonio Falzuni	1532-33
Antonio Manduca	1533-34
Matteo de Falzone	1534-35
Matteo Falzuni	1535-36
Antonio Manduca	1536-37
Antonio Manduca	1537-38
Antonio Goffredo Inguanez	1538-39
Goffredo Inguanez	1539-40
Matteo de Falzone	1542

Antonio Manduca	1543
Vincenso Vasco	1547
Antonio Inguanez	1549
D. Girolamo d'Alagona	1551
Matteo Falzon	1558
D. Antonio de Guevara	1564
Matteo Falzone	1566
Antonio de Guevara	1569
Alfonso Giovanni de Nava	1571
D. Francesco d'Alagona	1572
D. Giuseppe de Nava	1574
Alfonso Petri de Nava	1575
D. Ferdinando de Guevara	1577
Francesco d'Alagona	1579
Ferrante de Guevara	1580
Salvatore Montagnes	1581
D. Francesco d'Alagona	1582
Alfonso de Nava	1583
Gregorio Xerri Cicciano	1585
Ugolino Navarra	1588
Giovanni Maria Cassia	1591
Gregorio Xerri Cicciano	1593
D. Pietro de Guevara	1596
Ambrogio Falzon	1598
Anton Inguanez	1599
Gregorio Xerri Cicciano	1600
Pietro de Guevara	1602
Giovanni Domenico Xerri	1604
Gregorio Xerri Cicciano	1606
Michele Cassar	1610
Gregorio Xerri Cicciano	1612
Giovanni Maria Cassia	1614
Gregorio Xerri	1616
Gregorio Xerri Cicciano	1619
Antonio Cumbo	1624
Giov. Domenico Felici	1625
Giov. Vincens. Castelletti	1626

Francesco Mamo	1628
Antonio Turrenzi	1630
Francesco Perticomati	1634
Diego Ferriolo	1636
Giac. Testaferrata de Robertis	1637
Diego Antonio Ferriolo	1639
Ignazio Bonici	1641
Lorenzo Cassar	1643
Silvestro Fiteni	1645
Pietro Cassar	1653
Gio. Batta Micallef	1654
Gregorio Bonnici	1655
Gio. Batta Micallef	1657
Antonio Xara	1659
Pietro Cassia	1660
Gio. Domenico Muscat	1661
Gio. Maria Cardona	1663
Antonio Xara	1665
Giacinto Macedonia	1669
Gio. Domenico Muscat	1670
Stanislao Xara	1672
Pietro Mompalao	1674
Giacinto Macedonia	1676
Alessandro Mompalao	1678
Antonio Xara	1679
Domenico Bonnici	1681
Pietro Mompalao	1683
Gio. Batta Bonnici	1685
Baldassare Teuma	1687
D. Mario Tetaferrata	1690
Gio. Gurgion	1693
Martino Anton. Perticomati	1699
Ant. Perticomati Bologna	1700
Calcerano Mompalao	1701
Fabrizio Testaferrata	1703
Marc. Anton Inguanez	1706
Cosmano Cassar	1710

Antonio Bonnici	1711
Marc. Ant. Inguanez	1714
Antonio Muscat	1716
Pietro Mompalao	1718
Marc. Ant. Inguanez	1722
Pie. Pao. Galea	1731
Ferdinando Castelletti	1734
Marc. Ant. Inguanez	1741
Reggent Salv. Manduca	1762
Gio. Franc d'Amico	1765
D.P. Sceberras Testaferrata	1776
Gregorio Bonnici	1798
Francesco Gauci	1799
Giovanni Francesco Sant	1801
Reggent Dr Gius. Bonnici	1814

THE MALTA RAILWAY
(1883-1931)

The Malta Railway began its working life at 3p.m. on the 28th February 1883, arriving in Mdina from Valletta at 3.25p.m.

"The Malta Railway Company" had been formed four years earlier with a capital of £60,000 in 6,000 shares of £10 each. The first Chairman was Mr. George Cavendish Taylor who was also a Director of the London, Chatham and Dover Railway and of the Halesowen, the Mersey and the Varna Railways in Great Britain.

The railway line started in Valletta, passed through Floriana, Hamrun, Birkirkara and Attard and ended at the Museum Station just outside Notabile (Mdina): a distance of some seven miles.

The line from Valletta had one single track and the gauge was 3 feet 3 3/8 inches wide. The Company started with four locomotives, three bought from Mannin Wardle and Co. Ltd. of Leeds, and the fourth from Black, Hawthorn and Co. Ltd. of Gateshread.

Each locomotive carried a driver and a fireman and each coach carried between 24 and 26 passengers. The locomotive livery was a dark olive green with black wheels and frames. During 1904 a record 960,000 passengers travelled by rail, but the Company ran into financial difficulties and the trains stopped running on the 1st April, 1890. The railway was taken over by the Government and reactivated on the 25th February, 1892. Competition from tramways and omnibuses was strong and the railway was forced to close down on the 31st March, 1931.

You can see the Museum Station (between Mdina and Mtarfa) if you walk out of Mdina from the gateway in Magazine Street. The railway tunnel next to the Station is used to grow mushrooms.

ACTS OF THE APOSTLES

Chapter 28

Sojourn in Malta

"After our escape we learned that the island was called Malta.

2. And the natives showed us no small kindness, for they kindled a fire and refreshed us all because of the rain that had set in, and the cold.

3. Now Paul gathered a bundle of sticks and laid them on the fire, when a viper came out because of the heat and fastened on his hand.

4. When the natives saw the creature hanging from his hand, they said to one another, "Surely this man is a murderer, for though he has escaped the sea. Justice does not let him live".

5. But he shook off the creature into the fire and suffered no harm.

6. Now they were expecting that he would swell up and suddenly fall down and die, but after waiting a long time and seeing no harm come to him, they changed their minds and said he was a god.

Many cured at Malta

7. Now in the vicinity there were estates belonging to the head man of the island, whose name was Publius, and he received us and entertained us hospitably for three days.

8. And it happened that the father of Publius was laid up

with fever and dysentery; but Paul went in, and after praying and laying his hands on him, he healed him.

9. After this all the sick on the island came and were cured.

10. And they honoured us with many marks of honour, and when we sailed, they provided us with such things as we needed.

11. We set sail after three months in an Alexandrian ship with the Twins on her figurehead which had wintered at the island."

Index